Feminist Perspectives on Spiritual Direction

Women At The Well

4\9)

Kathleen Fischer

PAULIST PRESS
New York/Mahwah

ACKNOWLEDGEMENTS

The materials reprinted in *Women at the Well* first appeared in the following publica-
tions and are reprinted with permission: The lines from "Integrity" are reprinted
from *THE FACT OF A DOORFRAME, Poems Selected and New, 1950-1984,* by
Adrienne Rich, by permission of the author and W. W. Norton & Company, Inc.
Copyright © 1984 by Adrienne Rich. Copyright © 1975, 1978 by W. W. Norton &
Company, Inc. Copyright © 1981 by Adrienne Rich.; "A Litany of Woman's Power"
by Ann M. Heidekamp, USA from *No Longer Strangers. A Resource For Women and
Worship,* edited by Iben Gjerding and Katherine Kinnamon, copyright 1983 World
Council of Churches Publications, Geneva, Switzerland.; "The God Tree" from
Imagine That, by Marlene Halpin, Dubuque, IA: Wm. C. Brown Company Pub-
lishers, 1982, pp. 63—64; Excerpt from "Unlearning to No Speak," copyright 1969,
1971, 1973 by Marge Piercy. Reprinted from *Circles on the Water,* by Marge Piercy,
by permission of Alfred A. Knopf, Inc.; from *My Mother's Body,* by Marge Piercy.
Copyright © 1985 by Marge Piercy. Reprinted by permission of Alfred A. Knopf,
Inc.; "Self-Blessing," from *Mother Wit: A Feminist Guide to Psychic Development,*
copyright 1981 by Diane Mariechild, published by The Crossing Press, Freedom,
Ca.; Excerpt from "Poem For South African Women," copyright June Jordan.
Reprinted from *Voices of Women: Poetry By and About Third World Women,*
Women's International Resource Exchange, 1981; Denise Levertov, *Breathing the
Water.* Copyright © 1987 by Denise Levertov. Reprinted by permission of New
Directions Publishing Corporation; Excerpt from "Conversations Between Here
and Home," copyright Joy Harjo. Reprinted from *Voices of Women: Poetry By and
About Third World Women,* Women's International Resource Exchange, 1981;
reprinted with permission from "With No Immediate Cause" from *Nappy Edges* by
Ntozake Shange, St. Martin's Press, Inc., N.Y. and Methuen, London.

Library of Congress Cataloging-in-Publication Data

Fischer, Kathleen, 1940—
    Women at the well : feminist perspectives on spiritual direction/
Kathleen Fischer.
    p. cm.
    Bibliography: p.
    ISBN 0-8091-3018-1 (pbk.) : $9.95 (est.)
    1. Women—Religious life. 2. Spiritual direction. 3. Feminism—
Religious aspects—Christianity. I. Title.
BV4527.F57   1988
253.5—dc19   88-25329
                                                              CIP

Published by Paulist Press
997 Macarthur Boulevard
Mahwah, New Jersey 07430

Printed and bound in the
United States of America

Contents

Introduction

This book grew out of several converging streams of personal experience. It evolved, first of all, out of my work with women in spiritual direction. While listening to these women explore their spiritual issues, I learned first-hand how deep and pervasive the results of sexism are in women's lives. At the same time, I saw the tremendous gifts and strengths women possess. How, I wondered, could spiritual direction help women heal this damage and release these powers?

Answers began to come from two different directions. Through my training and ongoing experience as a social worker and therapist, I became aware of encouraging developments in feminist psychology and feminist therapy. As a theologian and teacher, I learned from the discoveries of feminist biblical scholars and theologians. As I began integrating insights from these sources into my spiritual direction ministry, I was able to listen to women in a new way, making connections I had not made before and attending to what I had previously overlooked. It was clear to me how much more helpful this kind of spiritual direction could be to women.

In this book I want to show how a feminist perspective transforms both the context and the content of spiritual direction. I write for all those who work with women in spiritual direction and retreat settings. And I write for individual women themselves, and groups of women, who may wish to use this book as a guide for self-direction and prayer.

Since feminism has a variety of meanings, I want to clarify my own use of it in designating this book as feminist perspectives on spiritual direction. I understand feminism to be a world view, a lens through which we see the world and all its internal relationships. As such, feminism stands in contrast with sexism as a world view. Sexism gives us constricted perspectives on the natures of women and men. It has become so much a part of our consciousness that the way the church and society are presently structured seems to be the way things naturally are. With the support of religion, these structures even appear to be divinely ordained. The distortions of a sexist perspective are not evident until we switch to a fresh viewpoint.

Feminism provides a new way of seeing reality. It is an alternative world view which replaces the divisions intrinsic to sexism with models of wholeness for both women and men. Feminism is a vision of life emphasizing inclusion rather than exclusion, connectedness rather than separateness, and mutuality in relationships rather than dominance and submission. Feminism also entails the conviction that full individual development can take place only within a human community that is structured in justice. And so feminism works for social change.

Feminism takes many forms. Some feminists have found it necessary to leave behind the Jewish and Christian traditions, finding the sexism of these religions so pervasive as to be irredeemable. I fully understand the reasons for their choice. However, I write for those who want to be both feminist and Christian and who believe this is possible. Consequently, I rely most heavily on those streams of feminist thought which support such a dual identity.

As a comprehensive world view, feminism addresses all of human experience. It concerns men as well as women, and much of what I say in this book will be helpful to men's spirituality. However, I focus on spiritual direction with women for two main reasons. First, while sexism has harmed men as well as women, it has been much more detrimental to women. Second, most existing books on spiritual direction are written by men and from a male perspective. They do not take full account of women's experience. That is the dimension I wish to supply.

The term "spiritual direction" as I intend it should also be clarified. Spiritual direction is a conversation in which a person seeks to answer the question, "What is spiritual growth and how do I foster it in my life?" The exchanges that comprise a spiritual direction relationship focus on awareness of and response to God in one's life. But since God is the deepest dimension of *all* experience, the conversation will range over every area of existence. Spiritual direction concerns the movement of our entire lives in and toward God.

I am aware of the problematic nature of the term "spiritual direction." As many authors have pointed out, neither "spiritual" nor "direction" aptly describes what it has become today. Spiritual direction is not "spiritual" in the sense that it focuses on one compartment of life divorced from everyday concerns. Nor is it "direction" if that is understood as one person taking responsibility for another's life and telling that person what to do. I retain the term, as other writers have, because it is familiar and easily identifies the reality I wish to address and modify. Throughout the book, however, I use many of the terms currently being substituted for direction, and speak of spiritual friends, companions, and guides.

Feminism influences the treatment that follows in two ways. First, I bring a particular perspective to the topics almost always covered in discussions of spiritual direction: spiritual direction itself, models of Christian growth, the experience of God, the role of Jesus, modes of prayer, discernment. Second, I treat several topics which are of special significance to women but are usually not included in discussions of spiritual direction. These are power, anger, violence against women, and women's spiritual legacy.

At the end of each chapter I offer suggestions for prayer and reflection. I see these as integral to the spiritual direction process, as they enable women to root that process deeply in

3

their experience. The exercises are designed to be used in both one-on-one and group spiritual direction contexts, or in retreat settings. Except where otherwise indicated, these are exercises I have developed myself for individuals and groups.

I am grateful to all of the women who have taught me through our spiritual direction conversations and who enrich this book with their experience. When referring to these women, I have changed identifying details in order to protect confidentiality. I also want to thank the women and men in my courses on Feminism and Christian Spirituality for helping me both confirm and revise my convictions. They showed me how difficult and painful, but also how renewing and life-giving, it is to integrate these convictions into personal experience. I am deeply grateful also to more than seventy-five women of various ages and backgrounds from throughout the United States who filled out questionnaires for me on their spirituality. Their statements appear throughout the book.

The New Testament uses a variety of images to depict the coming of a new humanity. These images—a woman in process of giving birth; yeast becoming bread; all persons living, moving, and finding their being in the cosmic womb of God— describe a process occurring not only within each individual but also within all of creation. I write out of a sense of the power spiritual friendships can have in bringing about the new creation.

1

Spiritual Direction in a Feminist Context

Spiritual direction has taken many forms throughout history. It has been shaped not only by major shifts in theology and spirituality, but also by the personal styles of individual directors such as Julian of Norwich, Catherine of Siena, Ignatius of Loyola, John of the Cross, and Teresa of Avila. In the midst of these varied emphases, however, a central focus has remained constant. The goal of spiritual guidance is openness and responsiveness to God's presence in our lives. Spiritual direction is a conversation in which a person gives expression to her experience of faith and discerns its movement.

As in the past, so today fresh theological and spiritual impulses are transforming the spiritual direction context. Chief among these are the insights of feminist theologians, spiritual writers, and therapists. In light of their challenge, it is clear that spiritual friendship will not meet the needs of women unless it reflects an awareness of the cultural and religious situation in which women find themselves and an acknowledgement of the harmful effects of the sexist society in which we live. This chapter will develop three implications of these feminist insights for the meaning and practice of spiritual direction: (1) a focus on women's experience as the authoritative starting point for spirituality; (2) the importance of recognizing the social as well as personal roots of women's spiritual issues; (3) the need to demystify the power relationship inherent in any helping process. A final section will discuss circles of women or women's groups as a form of spiritual companionship especially suited to the needs of women today.

WOMEN'S EXPERIENCE AS AUTHORITATIVE STARTING POINT

Attentiveness to a person's experience is, of course, central to any spiritual direction context. A spiritual guide helps a person lift into awareness and clarify aspects of her life which she might not otherwise notice. What a feminist perspective adds to this emphasis is belief in the authority of women's experience, confidence that we are engaged in a new encounter with the divine through that experience, and the conviction that it is a norm for the truthfulness of the tradition.[1] In its appeal to experience feminist spirituality affirms that all theology is dependent on a standpoint: it arises from the faith experience of particular individuals and communities. Feminism makes the additional claim that woman's experience is important for understanding God's revelation. In the past women have been excluded from shaping the theological tradition; it has, in fact, been used against them. Scripture and theology have been formed by male experience, not human experience.

As women reflect critically on their struggle for full human dignity and personhood, they recognize a contradiction between the tradition's interpretation of their identity and function and their own understanding of themselves and their lives. When symbols, texts and laws lose their ability to illumine and interpret experience, they become lifeless and lose their power. They must be given new meaning. Women interacting with their heritage out of their own experience are able both to free themselves from the sexism of the tradition and to bring new meaning to its symbols and texts. Like other liberation theologies, feminist theology holds that as those in

6

subordinate positions in society learn to trust themselves, they will find the courage to challenge prevailing definitions of reality and to work for the fashioning of a new creation.

In her novel, *Their Eyes Were Watching God*, Zora Neale Hurston conveys the power of uncovering women's experience. She traces one woman's journey, a black woman named Janie. Janie's self is a jewel inside her, but "covered over with mud." Janie reflects:

> When God had made The Man, he made him out of stuff that sung all the time and glittered all over. Then after that some angels got jealous and chopped him into millions of pieces, but still he glittered and hummed. So they beat him down to nothing but sparks but each little spark had a shine and a song. So they covered each one over with mud.[2]

Janie's story is her struggle against the forces that cover her jewel with mud and stifle her singing. These forces are both those encountered by black people and those experienced by women. Her life, thoughts, feelings and words are unified as she tells her story to her listening friend, Phoeby. Janie lives first out of her grandmother's dream for her and is angry at her grandmother for having "taken the biggest thing God ever made, the horizon . . . and pinched it to such a little bit of a thing." She finally finds herself and her voice by working through and transcending these limiting images.

Like Janie, women need someone who will hear their stories *on their own terms* and help them find their own horizons. A spiritual director can provide this kind of listening, but it requires awareness of the ways in which women have internalized the dominant cultural myths.

The skill of listening is the basis for spiritual companionship with both men and women; but in the case of women the quality of this listening is crucial. Women have long lived in the intervals between their inchoate experiences and the definitions given to experience by the stories of men. They have sensed vaguely that there is another truth buried in their own stories, but have not been able to find a language for it. Some part of them knows, whether they can articulate it or not, that many theological and spiritual notions fail to fit their situations. A basic tenet of feminist spirituality is the conviction that women have been socialized to discount their own feelings and responses. The power to name and identify reality has been held by men, who have described holiness and sinfulness for women based on their own male experience.

Consider, for example, the way sin and salvation have been defined by men according to their experience. Over two decades ago Valerie Saiving made this point.[3] Contemporary theology, she contends describes the human predicament as arising from separateness and the anxiety it occasions. Human freedom then brings with it the fear for the survival of the self and its values. Sin is the attempt to overcome this anxiety by magnifying our own power and knowledge. Love, on the other hand, is complete self-giving. Setting aside our own interests, we seek the good of others. Within this perception of the situation, sin is identified with self-assertion and love with self-lessness. Saiving challenges the validity of this definition for women, whose closeness to nature and cultural role of nurturing lead to a different kind of sin: lack of a clear sense of self, too much self-abnegation, diffuseness, and preoccupation with the trivial. However, spiritual literature is filled with a repetition of the traditional schema on sinfulness, and women's perspective is lost.

One metaphor used to convey this loss is that of "voice": women's voices have not been heard; individual women struggle to find their own voices. Marge Piercy describes this experience in her poem, "Unlearning to Not Speak":

> She must learn again to speak
> starting with I
> starting with We
> starting as the infant does
> with her own true hunger
> and pleasure
> and rage.[4]

The first step in spiritual direction therefore is helping a woman notice key experiences and bring them to speech. Its goal is discovery and awareness.

A young woman just three months pregnant talked about others' attempts to describe for her how she should feel. She was frequently nauseous and felt wretched, but a minister at the church where she worked persisted in saying that she had the glow of an expectant mother, and must be feeling fulfilled. She finally told him that it was actually a difficult time for her. What she was really working on in her own spiritual life was the meaning of pregnancy as a covenant, similar to God's covenant with us, where there is commitment and promise in the context of an unknown future. Her response was much deeper and more complex than the stereotypical notions of what a pregnant mother should feel. She reread the account of the annunciation and said that she understood immediately why Mary went first to Elizabeth. When she had learned that she was pregnant she had wanted to talk to other women, to listen to their experience.

Another woman in spiritual direction was trying to discern the meaning of Christian love in a relationship. What she heard from her partner in the relationship was that she was primarily to blame for what was going wrong. While willing to accept her own failures to love well, she was beginning to see that her partner's interpretation was not the whole story, that it was a rerun of the common version of the Adam and Eve story. She was growing in her ability to listen to the truth of her own perceptions rather than the distorted messages of centuries regarding woman as source of sin and evil. What a spiritual director does or says at this point can either confirm the authority of the woman's own truth, or affirm again the power of established conceptual schemes in her life. Such schemes—sin as pride and self-centeredness, holiness as obedient sonship—fail to help women make sense of their experience. If a spiritual director moves quickly to suggest such schemes, they will extinguish women's experience. Women will not be freed to see God in their lives as they actually do, but only according to previously sanctioned models.

Because a woman's experience may be fragile and buried beneath layers of traditional interpretations, another skill is essential to spiritual direction: listening with the imagination. The imagination knows the language of mystery and the sacred; revelation comes first at this level. Moreover, symbols and images operate preverbally and prerationally. They provide access to levels of experience deeper than, but not yet able to be formulated in, clear concepts. The new spirituality of women will first appear in these forms, and that is why the language of the imagination—image, symbol, story, dream, and ritual—is so important for spiritual guidance with women.[5]

Storytelling is the most spontaneous and basic way of naming experience. It is also an ancient and honored tool for preserving the wealth and variety of experience. One task of spiritual friends is to help women find the images that link their faith stories. Many women find it helpful to describe their spiritual experiences in terms of key images. Here are some that different women identify as most significant for them.

> The seashell is very important to me as symbolizing the rebirth and recommitment that I believe has taken place many times in my lifetime.

> I love the Tree of Life because of its inclusiveness and the process of growth conveyed by its flower and seed symbolism.

> My key religious experiences cluster around images of nature—ocean, waterfalls, mountains, deserts, clouds, and trees.

> Gardens are an important symbol for me. The Garden of Eden and all garden stories. My own garden is definitely a mystical place of beauty and inspiration.

> The monarch butterfly (caterpillar, chrysallis, and

10

butterfly stages) speaks to me of the paschal mystery
in my life.

At times women are aware of these images and symbols and
their importance in their faith stories. At other times the images occur spontaneously and can be missed. That is when the
spiritual guide who is listening with the imagination can be
especially helpful.

One woman, for example, in talking about her spirituality
said: "My life is swiss cheese. There are all these holes in it
where I don't have any experience at all." Exploring that spontaneous image helped her understand some of her longings and
frustrations. Another woman who was going through a painful
period in her life said, "I feel like a porcelain doll. If somebody
touched me or pushed me off the shelf, I'd break into a million
pieces." An older woman who had suffered a serious stroke
was struggling to find her way back to hope and trust in God.
In the course of one of our conversations, she said: "I feel like
there is a black wall in front of me, and a curtain that never
rises." When I asked her if she could think of any way in which
the curtain could be lifted, she said: "I guess if there were some
friends to help, it might be possible." Listening with the imagination supports a woman's process of befriending an image
and hearing its revelation. A spiritual guide can speak in terms
of the image, help a woman enter into, linger with it, let it
make its own connections, and learn what it has to teach her.
A good way to do this is to have her close her eyes and allow
the image to develop.

Along with stories and images, dreams and rituals are key
imaginative forms for expressing women's experience. One
woman says of her dreams:

Dreams have been very important in my spiritual life:
the woman with the skirt made of night sky who was
a powerful leader and risk taker; the warm and throb-
bing heart which grew and expanded to include more
and more people; the descent into the foggy river valley, connecting/linking with others to reach the other

11

side; a repeat of the same dream but finding ourselves
in muck, naming it and getting out.

Dreams are sources of revelation, and contain our personal
mythologies. Most spiritual guides have developed numerous
suggestions for listening to the language of dreams: keeping a
dream journal in which we record our dreams, walking around
in our dreams, completing the dream, sharing our dreams in a
group, noting the patterns of repetition that emerge in succes-
sive dreams, becoming the symbols in our dreams or asking
them questions, such as "Who are you?" "What do you represent in me?" Ritual, likewise, is a way in which women can
recognize their experiences and name them. Ritual embodies
our stories in symbol and action as well as in word and narrative. It also transforms our minds and spirits, and provides
meaning for our lives. Both listening to dreams and creating
rituals are integral dimensions of the spiritual direction process.

One of the first elements of a feminist perspective on spiritual guidance, then, is this respect for women's experience. A
helpful metaphor for spiritual direction, which takes account
of this emphasis, is spiritual director as *midwife*. In their study
of *Women's Ways of Knowing*, which is addressed primarily to
the field of education, the authors speak of the teacher as midwife. Women, they say, believe that they possess latent knowledge, and they yearn for teachers who will help them articulate
and expand this knowledge.

Given confirmation, they felt they could "just do anything." Lacking it, as one woman said, they were
"crippled" and "just can't function." Most of the
women we interviewed made it clear that they did not
wish to be told merely that they had the capacity or
the potential *to become* knowledgeable or wise. They
needed to know they already knew something (although by no means everything), that there was
something good inside them. They worried that there
was not.[6]

The authors note that for women, confirmation and community are prerequisites of growth. Their comments on the role of teachers hold true for spiritual directors as well. As one woman said of her experience of spiritual direction: "I need so much affirming. I need to experience ways of feeling that God and I are OK together, maybe not so much to hear that God loves me but that *SHE* likes me as I am."

A spiritual director as midwife assists women in giving birth to their own experiences, in making those experiences explicit so that they can develop and act on them. Women themselves indicate that this is what they value in spiritual direction. They describe helpful spiritual directors in this way:

> She helped me recognize and affirm my own spirituality.

> He has enabled me to grow by encouraging me to stretch, seek and stand up for what I believe.

> She totally accepts me for who I am, unconditionally.

> She listens to my questions, insights, desires; she offers prayer, love, affirmation, and suggestions to further assist me in my growth.

Newborn experiences may be fragile, easily crushed and denied. The spiritual director helps to see that they come to life with their truth intact.

This means renewed emphasis on the spiritual guide as one who learns from a person's own truth, who finds that person's strengths and enables her to build on them. As Madonna Kolbenschlag says in speaking of the characteristics of feminist spirituality,

> Women today are discovering that spirituality is authentic when it is intrinsically subjective, when it is brought forth, painfully, from the womb of their own experience. They are creating a new "wisdom literature" out of the alchemy of their own lives.[7]

It is difficult to find language and images for a consciousness that is just coming into being. It takes time and courage.

A spiritual director's capacity to listen in this way and to assist in the birth of new consciousness arises from awareness of the impact of oppression on women's lives. From a feminist perspective, doing spiritual direction with women includes a commitment to learning about women's issues and to becoming increasingly sensitive to their influence on the spiritual lives of individual women. It demands as well a willingness to have one's own spiritual categories challenged by the actuality of women's experience as they describe it.

THE SOCIAL ROOTS OF WOMEN'S SPIRITUAL ISSUES

Although the concept of spiritual direction has undergone numerous revisions in modern times, its historical roots lie in the movement of desert monasticism. Later, in the West, it became closely associated with the confessional. Because of these influences, as well as the privatistic bias that has marked spirituality generally, spiritual direction has traditionally focused on personal rather than social or political issues. A feminist perspective, along with other movements in contemporary spirituality, calls for a major shift in this focus.

First, feminism affirms the intrinsically social nature of spirituality. The ministry of spiritual guidance is one of liberation, enabling persons to move toward greater freedom and wholeness and challenging the structures that impede this. Personal and political issues are not unrelated; they are interwoven. Discernment must acknowledge the evil structures of the world and resist their impact. In *Soul Friend*, Kenneth Leech formulates well the questions raised for spiritual direction by such a shift in emphasis.

> Theology is at the heart of the question of the social relevance of direction. Is this ministry merely concerned with deepening a personal relationship of intimacy with Christ as Savior? Or is it concerned to deepen perception of the working of God in the struc-

14

tures of society? Is it concerned to enable individuals to live lives of devotion and piety within the accepted framework of the social order, or does it question the spiritual and moral values of that order? Adjustment to society, or the Kingdom of God—which is its perspective?[8]

A feminist perspective grows out of recognition of the harmful effects of oppression based on gender, class and race. It therefore sees the aim of spiritual direction not as adjustment, but rather as transformation based on a vision of the reign of God. A deepened life of contemplation, which is a goal of spiritual guidance, leads to a revolutionary vision of human life; it is the basis of resistance against all forms of evil.

Feminist therapy can provide helpful insights on this aspect of spiritual direction. A feminist approach to therapy grew out of a search for an alternative to traditional therapies which had failed to recognize the harmful effects of our sexist society and its tendency to perpetuate sex-role stereotypes. One of the key convictions of feminist therapy is that a person's emotional problems cannot be divorced from current social, historical and economic contexts. Speaking of therapy with Hispanic women, Guadalupe Gibson says:

> The focus has been on intrapsychic problems, with emphasis on changing the individual while ignoring the environment which often triggered the maladaptive behaviors.[9]

Feminist therapy rejects models which locate the source of human conflict within individuals, with no relationship to the larger social systems within which they live. In *A New Approach to Women and Therapy*, Miriam Greenspan calls such traditional therapy

> all the more destructive to women, who are encouraged by it to see the socially produced symptoms of sexual inequality as their own solely individual pathology. This kind of self-condemning internaliza-

15

tion is, in fact, a major aspect of the psychosocial oppression of women.[10]

From a social perspective it is not surprising that women in a male-dominated culture develop symptoms of powerlessness such as depression and low self-esteem. Theories that locate all problems within the individual end up blaming the victim. Traditional therapy, Greenspan believes, tells women that they will understand their personal problem by searching their personal history. In fact, for the real roots of the problem we must look beyond our personal histories to our history as women in society. This focus on social context applies to spiritual direction as well.

Some examples may help to indicate the importance of this shift in viewpoint. A number of the women I see in spiritual direction begin their description of an experience with phrases such as, "Something must be the matter with me" or "I don't know what's wrong with me," and then go on to talk about a conflict they are experiencing. The rest of the account may relate to any area—prayer, ministry, relationships, or family life: "Something must be the matter with me; I can't seem to get along with this parish team." Or, "I don't know what is wrong with me; I just don't enjoy reading scripture the way I used to." With such phrases these women express their belief that the problem lies somehow within them. Other women come to spiritual direction torn by the conflicting demands they feel in trying to be a good wife, a good mother, and at the same time fill well a role as teacher, scientist or artist, if they have chosen a profession. They blame themselves for their inadequacy instead of seeing their situation as the result of the conflicting demands placed upon women in our society. In this way women internalize the belief system that results from living in and accepting an oppressive state.

Spiritual direction can help women to stop blaming themselves, and learn instead to restructure their beliefs about themselves and their life situations in light of the reality of oppression. A woman's conflict with a parish team may be a result of the powerlessness she feels as a woman in an unjust situation rather than an indication of personal inadequacy.

16

Her problem with reading scripture may be a response to a growing awareness of the sexist nature of many biblical passages, not a spiritual failure on her part. It could also be a sign that God is not speaking to her primarily in scripture at a given time, and she needs encouragement to trust her experience. Spiritual direction done within a feminist framework will involve analysis of the social situation in order to help women differentiate between internal and external sources of conflict.

Within such a perspective spiritual directors become prophetic and imaginative guides. They are prophetic insofar as they make a vision of the reign of God the norm for change in the spiritual direction context. They name the evils that obscure and obstruct that reign, whether these evils take the form of exclusive male metaphors for God that undercut women's equal sacredness, church practices that deny women full participation, or patterns of relationship that keep women in dependent positions.

Spiritual direction, if done from a feminist perspective, also implies a commitment on the part of spiritual directors to work for the kinds of changes that will bring about equality for women. If the personal and political cannot be separated for the person seeking spiritual direction, neither can they be separated for persons engaged in the ministry of spiritual direction. That ministry concerns not simply the spiritual needs of individual women, but the spiritual interests of women as a whole. Beyond that, it is a ministry aimed at a new world view and its practical consequences. Anyone engaged in spiritual direction is continually called to conversion in this area.

A spiritual director is an imaginative as well as prophetic guide. One role of an imaginative guide is to help generate alternatives. Such alternatives have been seriously limited for women in many areas, their horizons narrowed. As a consequence, the recognition that present choices—images of God, styles of ministry, patterns of relating, forms of family life—are no longer adequate can lead to fear and despair. Without support that they can trust, women may be afraid to try out alternatives, or may find it impossible to believe there are alternatives. Spiritual direction can be an occasion for opening up new horizons, for expanding the range of choices available to a woman. It can generate resources that give rise to hope and a sense of possibility.

Memory is another function of the imagination, and an imaginative companion is one who remembers not only the individual's personal story but the collective story of women: the stories of Eve and of Mary of Nazareth, of the trial of women as witches and the struggles of women reformers such as Elizabeth Cady Stanton. Such a companion is able to suggest connections between individual and collective stories. This is crucial for women because they need to be reconnected to the larger family of women, to learn how they are similar and different from other women, and to move beyond notions generated by the dominant culture.

SPIRITUAL DIRECTION AND ISSUES OF POWER

Most contemporary descriptions of the spiritual director avoid traditional images such as spiritual father, physician of souls, or spiritual master, because they evoke a confessor/penitent context, rely on a medical model of sickness and cure, or emphasize the expertise and authority of the director and the obedience and submission of the person being directed. A spiritual director is often referred to today as a spiritual friend, guide, partner or companion. William Barry and William Connolly express this new emphasis well in *The Practice of Spiritual Direction.*

> Spiritual direction is a helping relationship, but the help offered is more like that of a companion on a journey than of an expert who, before the journey begins, advises what roads to take and answers the traveler's questions.[11]

Such models indicate a more equal relationship between a director and the person coming for spiritual direction. From a theological viewpoint these images also reinforce the truth that it is the Spirit who guides us, and that all those in the spiritual direction context stand under the Spirit's ultimate claim and mystery.

This issue of models for spiritual direction is of special significance for women since they are already conditioned to see themselves as inferior and to rely on powerful authority figures, usually men. The myth of the expert is more harmful to women than it is to men. They have been taught that submission and obedience, not the appropriation of one's own spiritual gifts and power, are the paths to holiness. If a spiritual direction experience is to be liberating for women, its very process must counteract the dependence that is the fruit of oppression.

Biblical support for a more egalitarian model of spiritual direction can be found in Elisabeth Fiorenza's *In Memory of Her.* Obviously, Fiorenza is not writing about spiritual direction. She is, however, describing ministry in the Christian community and its original impulse in the Jesus movement of first century Palestine. She shows that this movement created a discipleship of equals, and that the Christian missionary movement spread this egalitarian lifestyle to Gentile territory, in open conflict with the predominant patriarchal ethos. The all-inclusive goodness of the God of Jesus breaks through the distinctions between those considered marginal persons and those seen as holy and righteous in Israel. In baptism all Christians become a Spirit-filled people.

> They are all equal, because they all share in the Spirit, God's power; they are all called elect and holy because they are adopted by God, without exception.[12]

As a form of Christian ministry, spiritual direction must be based on this model of the discipleship of equals, on the worth of all persons and the gift of the Spirit to all.

These theological considerations have practical implications. The first is that the process of spiritual guidance needs to be demystified. Some women still hold a sort of magical or idealized notion of the spiritual director which is a corollary to their own self-depreciation. It is important, then, to make clear that spiritual direction is a dialogue in which both persons are listening to the Spirit. Although there may be differences in knowledge, skills, and experience when persons come

19

together in a spiritual direction context, it is not a situation of expert and learner, or doctor and patient.

In other words, a woman should learn about her own power through the spiritual direction process as she maintains her own authority in the relationship, learns to love and trust herself, to know her own strength, and to extend her own capabilities and limits. Even if she begins the relationship with feelings of insecurity and dependence, in the end spiritual guidance is no longer seen or needed in the same way.[13]

Spiritual directors can do several things which will create greater mutuality in the spiritual direction situation.

(1) Establish an informal, nonhierarchical atmosphere by making the process of exploring and clarifying experiences, identifying concerns, offering suggestions, and evaluating results, a cooperative venture throughout.

(2) Disclaim the role of expert and introduce persons in spiritual direction to primary spiritual resources, i.e., writings on prayer, theories of spiritual growth, so that they are not dependent on the spiritual director for this knowledge. In this way the spiritual guide becomes a resource rather than an authority.

(3) Point out the limitations of spiritual direction itself. It is only one among many avenues for spiritual growth, and not essential for everyone.

(4) Avoid patterning the spiritual direction relationship on scientific models which hold that distance and objectivity are the prerequisites for healing and personal growth. This scientific model has been adopted by much traditional therapy, and Miriam Greenspan offers a critique of such therapy which applies to other helping settings.

> It is just this distance, the emotional withholding of the therapist, that is considered essential to his neutrality. Yet it is a male bias to think this is so. In fact, there is nothing more inherently neutral or scientific or professional about emotional distance than there is about emotional connection or nurturance. . . . Emotional give and take is a distinctively female style in our culture. The traditional approach takes its model

of expertise from the male style of personal inter-
course.[14]

Such emotional give and take is captured well in the model of
direction as friendship. It implies that a director is comfortable
with strong emotions in herself and others. She is able to give
and receive expressions of love and anger, and to work through
the complexities and ambiguities of these emotions.

(5) Recognize the reciprocity in the spiritual direction relationship. Spiritual companionship enriches the companion
and deepens her own faith; we receive many gifts from those
we accompany on their spiritual journeys and they need to
know they have given to us as well as received from us. When
spiritual direction is seen in terms of the meaning of relationships, it also becomes clear that what is good for a person is
not determined ahead of time, but emerges from the relationship itself.

NEW MODELS OF SPIRITUAL DIRECTION: WOMEN'S CIRCLES

Virginia Woolf once called the relationship between wom-
en "that vast chamber where nobody has been."[15] Women
are now beginning to explore that chamber. Recognizing the
importance of collaboration among women and the creative
potential of women's friendships and support groups, many
women have found companionship for their spiritual journey
in a circle of women rather than in one director. Women who
have been a part of such groups describe the experience in the
following ways.

It is a place to talk about our experience of God and
develop our own rituals.

I get hope from other women who listen to my story
and share theirs with me.

A group of seven women have listened to me and
loved me unconditionally. They have never turned

their backs on me, but more than that they see value in me. They have encouraged me to question attitudes and patterns in my life that are not conducive to wholeness.

Feminism has animated my religious faith and helped me rise to my full stature and claim my space in this patriarchic tradition. Of course, this causes conflict within myself (I can no longer be the nice person who jokes a lot about women's issues and whom my brothers treat like a kid sister). No, I have hard things to say and live in order to claim my space, and clear spaces for all of us. I do not expect it to get any easier, either. What I need to be true to my call (vocation) is the company of other women for support, prayer, challenge, and critical reflection.

As is apparent from these comments, the processes of spiritual direction take place in these groups: listening, clarifying, offering suggestions and alternate interpretations for experience, facilitating exercises that will help to draw out ideas and images, putting persons in touch with spiritual resources. In addition, such groups are based on women's unique strengths and world view.

This group approach to spiritual direction renews an emphasis that has long been a part of the tradition. In *Spiritual Friend. Reclaiming the Gift of Spiritual Direction*, Tilden Edwards calls group spiritual guidance the standard form of guidance in Christian tradition. Some of its current forms include groups gathered for faith sharing, scriptural reflection, singing, and prayer. As he notes, the richness of insight available in a group can outstrip that available in a one-to-one relationship; a group can also be more supportive and stimulating.[16] Adrian Van Kaam believes that group direction should be the norm in the church, with one-to-one direction reserved largely for crisis times:

(Private) direction is less common, not available to most Christians, filled with risks and by no means necessary for every person who wants to grow in the life of grace.[17]

Women are seeking spiritual support in both one-on-one and group spiritual direction, but, for many reasons, groups can be an especially helpful form of spiritual companionship for women:

(1) In a circle of women, giving and receiving can take place in a mutual way. One is no longer simply helper or person being helped, but both. This is true even in those groups where one person regularly serves as facilitator.

(2) Groups provide many opportunities for being understood and affirmed by other women. When stories of faith journeys are shared, women find that others have had experiences similar to theirs; this commonality of experience enables them to feel normal, to see the connections between their personal and cultural experiences. In the absence of such companionship, women often feel isolated, crazy and different.

(3) Many forms of prayer can be most effectively taught and learned in a circle or group. Most groups pray together as part of their gathering. Many women mourn the loss of liturgical expression that relates to their experience; they thirst for life-giving ritual. Groups can provide opportunities for symbolic expression that fill the void created by current sexist practice in the church. They enable women to experience inclusive language and alternate forms of prayer and worship.

Women continue to choose both one-on-one and group spiritual direction, depending on their own needs and inclinations. The emphases outlined in this chapter apply to either situation. Those emphases are: the importance of women's own experience, the social roots of women's spiritual concerns, and the rebalancing of power in helping relationships.

FOR PRAYER AND REFLECTION

Before moving to the exercises for this chapter, I want to give some general orientation to the exercises found throughout the book:

(1) A number of these exercises suggest that you begin by relaxing. We relax when we come to our senses. This can be done by concentrating on your body, moving in awareness from part to part, experiencing any physical sensations you pick up there, and then moving on.

Or, you can focus on your breathing. Close your eyes and breathe in and out deeply several times, then assume a more natural rhythm. Take in God's love as you breathe in, and let go of fears, tensions, anxieties, and all else that you want to let go of as you breathe out.

(2) Several are exercises in guided imagination. You can have someone lead you through these exercises individually or in a group, move through the exercise slowly yourself, or put the exercise on a tape recorder and play it back. They seem to go better when guided by someone else, but they can also be effective when you do them by yourself.

Remember to go slowly, allowing enough time between the steps. If you find one section particularly fruitful, stay with it and give it time to develop. The imagination is an important gift and source of revelation. It has its own language and dynamism, and speaks best when we do not try too hard. Simply relax and listen to whatever comes. If nothing seems to be happening, talk with your director or group about what was difficult and why. Since the imagination is closely tied to our emotions, you may experience deep feelings during these exercises. These are important parts of your experience, and it is often helpful to talk about them with your director or group.

Now the exercises for this chapter.

1. Some Ways to Begin Telling Your Story

a. *The Story of My Relationship with God*
   What God once was for me
   What God is for me now
   What I hope for from God's future
b. *Points of Entry into My Life Story*
   The experiences of my life which most tell me who I am
   The key transitions or passages in my life

My favorite verbs, metaphors, and adjectives

The most important images in my spiritual life

My personal myth: figures of good and evil, heroes and heroines

Works of art in which I find myself or which capture moments of my life for me

c. *My Story and Cultural Stories*

How my story relates to those groups and institutions to which I belong

2. Your Sexual Lifeline: A Journal Exercise

At times when telling your story, it is helpful to focus on one aspect of your life. For example, one woman discovered that music had been an important symbol in her life of faith. She recounted her life as a rich and varied musical score: early memories of her grandmother's perpetual singing of gospels and spirituals, her father singing the blues, hymns sung at church, music shared with friends and neighbors.

The following are suggestions for drawing your sexual lifeline by looking back over events in your life which contributed to your sexual identity. Begin with your earliest memory and think through each time period, recalling persons and experiences which shaped your understanding of your own sexuality. Consider:

a. the messages you received from others about being female: mother, father, brothers and sisters, church, school, friends, media.

b. early sexual experiences and their effect on you.

c. how you regarded your emerging body during adolescence.

d. how you reacted to sexual feelings.

e. any breakthroughs in loving and accepting your own body, and how these came about.

f. any breakthroughs in relating sexually to others.

3. Models of Spiritual Direction

Several metaphors for the spiritual director are suggested in this chapter: spiritual director as midwife, as prophetic guide, as imaginative companion. What is your own metaphor? Reflect on what it tells you about the way you see the director's role. What do you want to retain and change?

4. Spiritual Direction in Groups or Circles

The following are questions to consider as a group of women first comes together:

a. What is our purpose?
b. What arrangements do we want to make regarding the time and length of our meetings, the duration of the group, and our commitment to one another?
c. How will leadership be exercised in our group? One facilitator? Rotating leadership?
d. How will we assure confidentiality?
e. How can we create an atmosphere for spiritual growth— e.g., preserving a non-judgmental attitude, refraining from giving advice and problem-solving, incorporating prayer and ritual into our sessions?
f. Do we have referral sources if individuals uncover issues they want to explore further outside the group, or which the group feels it cannot or does not want to handle?

[1]See Letty M. Russell, *Household of Freedom. Authority in Feminist Theology* (Philadelphia: Westminster Press, 1987), pp. 30–33; and Mary Jo Weaver, "Enlarging the Borders of Our Language: The Promise of Feminist Theology," in *Miriam's Song* (Hyattsville, MD: Quixote Center, 1987), pp. 7–10.

[2](Urbana: University of Illinois Press, 1978), pp. 138–39.

[3]"The Human Situation: A Feminine View," in *Womanspirit Rising. A Feminist Reader in Religion*, ed. Carol P. Christ and Judith Plaskow (San Francisco: Harper & Row, 1979), pp. 25–42.

[4]*To Be of Use* (New York: Doubleday, 1973), p. 38.

[5]For further reflections on the role of the imagination in spirituality, see my discussion in *The Inner Rainbow. The Imagination in Christian Life* (New York: Paulist Press, 1983).

[6]Mary Field Belenky, Blythe McVicker Clinchy, Nancy Rule Goldberger, and Jill Mattuck Tarule, *Women's Ways of Knowing. The Development of Self, Voice, and Mind* (New York: Basic Books, 1986), p. 195. See also p. 217.

[7]"Feminists, the Frog Princess, and the New Frontier of Spirituality," in *New Catholic World* 225 (July/August, 1982), 160.

[8](San Francisco: Harper & Row, 1977), p. 188.

[9]"Hispanic Women: Stress and Mental Health Issues," in *Women Changing Therapy. New Assessments, Values and Strategies in Feminist Therapy*, ed. Joan Hamerman Robbins and Rachel Josefowitz Siegel (New York: Harrington Park Press, 1985), p. 123.

[10](New York: McGraw-Hill, 1983), p. 21. See also Susan Sturdivant, *Therapy with Women: A Feminist Philosophy of Treatment* (New York: Springer Publishing Co., 1980); and *Women and Psychotherapy: An Assessment of Research and Practice*, ed. Annette M. Brodsky and Rachel T. Hare-Mustin (New York: Guilford Press, 1980).

[11](Minneapolis: Winston-Seabury, 1982), p. 137. For a similar emphasis, see Thomas Hart, *The Art of Christian Listening* (New York: Paulist Press, 1980), and Katherine Marie Dyckman, S.N.J.M and L. Patrick Carroll, S.J., *Inviting the*

Mystic, Supporting the Prophet (New York: Paulist Press, 1981).

[12](New York: Crossroad Publishing Co., 1983), p. 199.

[13]This perspective is evident throughout Sandra Schneiders' comments in "The Contemporary Ministry of Spiritual Direction," in *Spiritual Direction. Contemporary Readings,* ed. Kevin G. Culligan, O.C.D. (Locust Valley, NY: Living Flame Press, 1983), pp. 41–56.

[14]*A New Approach to Women and Therapy,* p. 28.

[15]Quoted by Adrienne Rich in *On Lies, Secrets, and Silence: Selected Prose 1966–1978* (New York: W. W. Norton & Co., 1979), p. 199.

[16](New York: Paulist Press, 1980).

[17]*The Dynamics of Spiritual Self Direction* (Denville, NJ: Dimension Books, 1976), p. 384.

2

A New Vision
of Christian Growth

We seek spiritual direction in order to grow in the Christian life. Hence convictions about what constitutes such growth are crucial to the entire process. If growth is aimed at openness to the divine presence, what results can God's presence and activity be expected to produce? Just as therapy is shaped by models of human health and wholeness, so approaches to spiritual guidance are grounded in beliefs about the meaning of holiness or Christian maturity. These convictions may never be directly stated, but they are nonetheless present in every spiritual direction conversation, guiding it the way awareness of a destination influences travelers' decisions.

Because traditional models of holiness have been restrictive for women, they are being replaced by new ways of envisioning Christian growth. A feminist spirituality is evolving, one not yet fully articulated; it is arising out of the experience of women themselves as they reclaim traditions and create new ones.[1] Even in its initial formulation, however, it can change what we are attentive to and how we evaluate what is happening in our lives of faith. Further, awareness that we stand at the frontiers of a new spirituality for women enables us to contribute to its development.

Several of the major themes of this spirituality appear in a familiar gospel story. John's gospel tells of a Samaritan woman who comes to Jacob's well to draw water. Jesus, who is passing through Samaria, engages her in conversation. This conversation results in greater wholeness for the woman and a conviction that the divine life dwells within her. It is remarkable that the conversation takes place at all, for a Jew did not dare to address a Samaritan, a man did not speak to a woman in public. Jesus challenges this exclusive pattern of relationships; his disciples are shocked to find him revealing himself to a woman.

The conversation between the Samaritan woman and Jesus concerns her life and thirsts. Together Jesus and the woman explore different kinds of wells and water that might quench that thirst.

> *Jesus:* "Whoever drinks this water will thirst again; but whoever drinks the water that I give will never thirst again. The water that I give will become a spring within, welling up to eternal life."

> *The Woman:* "Give me this water, so that I may never thirst and never have to come here again to draw water" (Jn 4:13–16).

In the course of her meeting with Jesus, the Samaritan woman comes to believe that she has inside her a spring of living water, an unfailing source of life, the gift of the Spirit. The force of Jesus' revelation is such that it takes her back to her community, but with a new role within it. She is now a witness to the true meaning and promise of Jesus, as he has revealed it to her. The new power alive in this woman changes the faith of an entire Samaritan village.

Like the Samaritan woman, contemporary women thirst for living water. They stand at the well, hoping to draw life from ancient traditions. They long to discover their own inner wells, to meet God within, as source of their wisdom, power, creativity and strength. They want to be wellsprings of new vision and hope, to use their gifts to change their communities and the world community.

However, women today are also like the Samaritan woman in their experience of oppression and exclusion. In order to drink from their wells, they must challenge established cultural and religious beliefs. Like the Samaritan woman, they are beginning to see themselves and the world in fresh ways. Out of this awareness arises a call for a new spiritual vision which we will explore in its several aspects: (1) models of human wholeness to replace stereotypes of male and female holiness; (2) an affirmation of woman's sacredness to heal past devaluation of female experience; (3) a focus on interdependence to resolve the split between self and other in Christian spirituality; (4) inclusive categories of thought and action in place of the exclusive ones now so dominant; (5) the elimination of all interlocking forms of oppression.

As we examine each of these areas, it will become clear how they transform our conceptions of Christian growth. They have in common a concern for wholeness at all levels of human life. The specifics of their challenge will vary from person to person, and we will be exploring the practical implications for spiritual direction in subsequent chapters. What I am presenting here are the theoretical principles for all that follows.

MODELS OF HOLINESS

In her conversation with Jesus, the Samaritan woman finds both healing and a sense of her own sacredness. These are important spiritual goals for all women. Something of the thirst the Samaritan woman experiences before she meets Jesus at the well is conveyed by a novel that shows vividly how all kinds of oppression restrict human wholeness.

Harriette Arnow wrote *The Dollmaker* in 1954, but it has recently been revived. It is a novel about the killing of spirits, and the struggle to free imprisoned voices and faces. *The Dollmaker* is the story of Gertie Nevels, a big, self-reliant woman who is uprooted from the Kentucky hills and thrust into the confusion of wartime Detroit. At the beginning of the novel we see Gertie in Kentucky in her own world, knowing her strength, having faith in her audacity. In Detroit she becomes increasingly inarticulate. The message she hears is: Learn to be like the others. Learn to be like the others. To be saved in this culture one must remake oneself entirely.

Gertie is a whittler who makes beautiful wooden dolls. She has a piece of cherry wood which she wants to carve as the face of Christ. Throughout the novel Gertie dreams of the proper face for this Christ. She never locates that face. The Christly image she seeks is at once her own and that of millions of people, like herself, who might have been models for Christ. As Joyce Carol Oates says in the afterword to *The Dollmaker*, these Christly figures "do not emerge out of the wood, they do not become incarnated in time, they are not given a face or a voice. They remain mute, unborn."[2]

Works such as Arnow's remind us of how partial our images of human wholeness and holiness have been, distorted as they are by various forms of oppression. Men as well as women have been restricted in the ways they are allowed to experience and express reality. Sexism has led to limiting beliefs about the natures of women and men, dividing humanity into male and female and assigning characteristics accordingly: human persons are called to be either rational or emotional, spirit or body, active or passive. Traditional ideals of spiritual perfection reflect these stereotypical qualities, frequently resulting in portrayals of women saints as sentimental and submissive or urging women to imitate manly virtues as soldiers of Christ who are engaged in the spiritual struggles of Christian warfare. Feminist spirituality seeks to heal such dualisms and replace them with a vision of human wholeness for both women and men. In this way the faces and voices denied expression can come to life.

This approach to Christian growth requires a new theology of the person, one which affirms that all the truly significant spiritual qualities are attainable by both women and men. Those attempting to develop this understanding of the person face an unanswered question: Beyond biological differences, are women and men fundamentally the same or different? In other words, are differences between the sexes socially constructed or biologically determined? The answer to this question remains unsettled among feminists themselves, and the extent to which differences between the sexes are natural or cultural may only be resolved, if it ever is, by further anthropological and cultural research.

While on this topic of male and female differences, it is important to note that from the perspective of many feminists, Carl Jung's anima/animus theory is problematic. Jung called the opposites in man and woman the anima and animus. By the anima he meant the feminine component in a man's personality, and by the animus he meant the masculine component in a woman's personality. Jung's system has influenced many areas of Christian spirituality, but as a number of critics have pointed out, his approach continues to support a vision of the human based on polarities, supporting the idea that there are perpetual masculine and feminine principles in the human psyche. This legitimates the notion of incompleteness in male and female.

While Jung's anima/animus theory may address the situation of men in ways helpful to them, it continues the notion that woman's completeness comes in terms of the male. For Jung the feminine is biological, innate, even ontological. In her recent careful study of *Jung and Feminism*, Demaris S. Wehr concludes that Jung's male-centeredness and distrust of women distort his discussion of the anima and animus, and the feminine. Because of Jung's cultural and gender bias, analytical psychology does not contain an adequate definition of women and the feminine. Consequently, she says:

> Women readers and analysands need to recognize and challenge these elements of Jung's psychology or it will remain a seductive trap, luring them with compelling images of the 'feminine', and thereby contributing to our lack of awareness of the internalized oppression that can be fostered by use of his categories.[3]

While feminists criticize Jung's categories of feminine and masculine, his psychology makes many important contributions to the spiritual lives of women and men. Among these is his vision of the importance of myth, ritual, symbol and dream in human life.

Biological differences between women and men are important; because of living in and through a female body, women have experiences of the world which men do not have. But these biological differences have been defined by men and used as the basis for social and cultural constructions of what is male and female, constructions which support male dominance and female inferiority. Research indicates how difficult it is to identify any personality traits as innately masculine or feminine; in many areas, differences within each sex may be greater than differences between the sexes.[4] In this regard, I have been repeatedly struck by the fact that whenever I have asked a class on spirituality to list what they consider to be masculine and feminine qualities, we invariably end with both women and men arguing that there is no attribute they would necessarily exclude from their spiritual lives.

While it is not possible to divide human experience into innate male and female traits, it is possible to discuss the differences in male and female behaviors and values which have developed from the impact of cultural forces. These differences do exist and have been translated into dominant and subordinate positions in society, thereby excluding women from the definition of the fully human that maleness has come to represent. The male is the center of experience, and we have become accustomed to thinking about ourselves, the world, and all that is in the world from the male perspective. Since maleness is normative women must choose between being fully human adults and retaining the so-called feminine characteristics that are assigned to women by church and society and guarantee women's acceptance.

Other practical consequences result from this marginal status of women. Qualities that have been designated as feminine behavior—care, nurturing, receptivity, emotion, imagination, relationality, and self-sacrifice—have been devalued and excluded from a major role in the public sphere. One aspect of the present movement toward wholeness for women and men is restoring the importance of these qualities and integrating them into the lives of all persons and all aspects of existence.

In terms of spiritual growth, stereotypical qualities have acquired special power from their embodiment in traditional figures of holiness. Women appropriate and live out of these images at deep levels. Part of spiritual friendship is helping women identify and choose the models they want to influence their spiritual growth. Comparison of two ways of speaking of the holiness of Mary of Nazareth illustrates the way these models incorporate female stereotypes and how they are being transformed. The first description of Mary is from a 1966 address of Paul VI on the meaning of womanhood.

> For us, woman is a vision of virginal purity, which restores the most lofty affective and moral feelings of the human heart. For us, she is, in man's loneliness, the arrival of his companion who knows the supreme gift of love, the value of cooperation and help, the strength of fidelity and diligence, the common heroism of sacrifice. For us, she is the Mother—let us bow our heads—the mysterious source of human life, where nature still receives the breath of God, the creator of the immortal soul. . . . For us, she is mankind . . . which, whether it sings, prays, sighs or weeps, seems thus naturally to converge toward a unique and supreme, spotless and sorrowful figure, the privileged woman, blessed among all women, the Virgin, Mother of Christ, Mary.[5]

This is the image many Roman Catholic women grew up with, Mary as idealized Virgin and Mother, model of the virtues of humility and selfless devotion.

A second description of Mary shows how she is now being viewed by some women in terms of the universal quest for wholeness and liberation. It is from an address by Julia Esquivel, an exiled Guatemalan teacher and poet, who lectures and works for human rights in Central America. She speaks of the struggle for a new world and says of Mary:

> Mary, the young peasant from Nazareth, is a para-
> digm for all women who have faith and hope for a new
> society in which human life is the most sacred value.
> Engaged to an artisan, Mary was preparing herself for
> a married life. But the intervention of the God of the
> poor superseded that dream and project for something
> larger, a plan for her own people and for all of human-
> ity.[6]

Mary's acceptance of God's project of transformation for her people was, Esquivel believes, like a sword piercing her heart until the true meaning of her life became clear. Her example leads us to reflect on our own deepest motivations for sharing in the struggle for women's liberation. Mary of Nazareth, like Catherine of Siena and Dorothy Day, becomes a model of prophetic freedom.

Fresh images of woman's holiness are healing the imaginations of Christian women. These models challenge prevailing stereotypes of male and female, replacing them with wholeness as the goal of Christian growth for both women and men.

WOMEN AND THE SACRED

One dimension of the wholeness women seek is belief in their own sacredness and capacity to image the divine. It is important to recognize here that it is basic to conceptions of Christian growth for women. Women need to find the divine principle, the saving power at their center in order to believe finally in their own worth. The Samaritan woman recovered this during her meeting with Jesus at the well, when she learned that she had within her a spring of living water.

Water is a biblical symbol for God. As the prophet Isaiah writes:

That day,
sing of the delightful vineyard!
I, God, am its keeper;
every moment I water it
for fear its leaves should fall;
night and day I watch over it
(Is 27:2–3; see also Ps 46:4;
Is 41:18, 44:3–4, and 58:11).

As a symbol for the divine presence and activity, water is associated with growth and renewal. Its free gift is liberation.

O, come to the water all you who are thirsty;
though you have no money, come! (Is 55:1).

The Samaritan woman's discovery that there is within her a spring of living water is Jesus' affirmation that at the center or core of her being, she is holy and a bearer of holiness. Her well within is a font of liberation.

Women spiritual writers also see water as a symbol for the God at the center of their being. In *The Interior Castle*, Teresa of Avila uses water to image the entire life of the spirit. The symbol of water conveys her awareness of God's deep interior presence within and the hidden riches and depths of the human person. She says,

For I don't find anything more appropriate to explain some spiritual experiences than water; and this is because I know little and have no helpful cleverness of mind and am so fond of this element that I have observed it more attentively than other things.[7]

Teresa compares different kinds of prayer to the way in which two fountains with two different basins are filled with water. The way of active meditation is like filling the basin through the use of much ingenuity in bringing water from far away. This kind of prayer begins with the person and ends in God. In infused prayer, the source of the water is right there and fills

37

the basin noiselessly. This prayer begins with God and ends in the person. Water is always flowing from the spring.

A similar image is found in the diaries of a young Jewish woman who died at Auschwitz in November of 1943 at the age of twenty-nine. Etty Hillesum composed these diaries during the last two years of her life, but they have only recently been discovered and published as *An Interrupted Life.*[8] Her daily reflections reveal not only her intellectual passions and growing understanding of her sexuality, but an independent and vibrant young woman's journey to new spiritual depths. At the heart of this journey is her thirst for prayer. In one of her diary entries she says that there is a really deep well inside of her, and in it God dwells. Sometimes she is there too. But often stones and grit block the well and God is buried underneath. Gradually, however, she learns to draw on this well to give her courage and to center her being.

Etty's diaries witness to another dimension of women's quest for the sacred; they show how she integrates her body and sexuality with her spirituality. Her diary entries reveal the interweaving of her erotic feelings with her search for an authentic relationship with God. She sees her body as a source not of sinfulness, but of wonder. Sexuality has often been a principle of division in the spiritual realm, with flight from the body viewed as synonymous with pursuit of the spirit. This is another result of the sexual dualism that has marked much of the Christian tradition. Not only has spirit been opposed to body, but spirit has been assumed to be higher and superior, the body lower and inferior. Men identified themselves with the spirit or mind and identified women with the body or matter. Within such a dualistic system, the goal becomes control of mind over body.[9]

In view of this history, the goal of Christian growth is to experience our sexuality again as a source of unity and healing, reunited with the experience of the sacred. Woman's bodily existence is not peripheral to, let alone detrimental to, our spiritual becoming; it is central to it. Philosopher Charlene Spretnak shows that sexuality is the energy of our relating to everyone and everything.

> The experiences inherent in women's sexuality are expressions of the essential holistic nature of life on Earth; they are *body parables* of the profound oneness and interconnectedness of all matter/energy.[10]

Spretnak calls on women to reclaim menstruation, pregnancy, childbirth, motherhood, and menopause. Doing so as Christian women means asking what these experiences tell us about our experience of God and the living out of the gospel. This calls for a reversal of the sexual taboos which have declared woman's body to be religiously unclean and a barrier to the sacred. One of the goals many women have in spiritual direction is to experience themselves as body/spirit unities and to view their bodies as holy and an avenue to the sacred.

A related spiritual direction task is challenging the myth of the half-person. Society has taught women to believe that their sexuality exists only in relation to and in dependence on men, that men will make them whole. Women face this societal norm, often revealed in the comments of family members or friends, as they struggle to affirm their lesbian orientation, their decision to remain single, or their desire for full personhood in marriage or when widowed or divorced. Christian growth aims at replacing this notion that woman's sexual identity is incomplete and reflective with convictions about its wholeness and sacredness. This is one aspect of Christian reconciliation—bringing together elements that have been torn apart by the sin of sexism.

AN INTERDEPENDENT WORLD

The Samaritan woman emerges from the gospel account as both free and related. She shows concern for relationships, but this does not diminish her capacity for self-direction. Women have traditionally been led to believe they must choose between caring for self and nurturing relationships. They cannot have both. Such a dilemma derives once again from a dualistic world view which separates individual and relational elements of existence. This dichotomy suggests that no one can be both fully an individual and fully related. And so individuality is usually assigned to men, relatedness to women. Men are taught that they are, or should be, essentially self-directing and autonomous; women, that they should serve the needs of others, especially husband and children. However, this service has been given less cultural value than male self-direction and autonomy.

In *Habits of the Heart,* Robert Bellah and his colleagues describe the belief system of the majority of Americans as ontological individualism, a conviction that the basic unit of reality is the autonomous individual who *subsequently* decides about being related. When we choose to be related, we do so either for utilitarian reasons—it will be useful—or for expressive reasons—it expresses my affection or my esteem.[11] This prevailing American view fosters a very disconnected interpretation of the individual.

Feminist spirituality seeks to replace this dichotomy with a vision of mutuality in which individuality and relatedness are compatible and necessary aspects of all reality, supporting and enhancing one another. New descriptions of holiness for women include the virtues of self-esteem and independence as well as those of relationality and care for others. At the heart of reality is a mutual rhythm of giving and receiving, the receiving of others for the enrichment of self and the giving of self for the enrichment of others. As Dorothee Soelle says in *The Strength of the Weak. Toward a Christian Feminist Identity,*

> this net of giving and taking is part of our daily experience. Every time we learn to give without calculating what we will get in return and every time we learn to receive without feeling ashamed or indebted, we tie a few more knots into this large net and make it a little more secure.[12]

Such a perspective enables women and men to transcend a spirituality that would require unlimited self-sacrifice of women while allowing assertiveness and self-interest in men.

It also situates the problem women experience, not in the notion of self-sacrifice as such, but in the fact that self-sacrifice is considered primarily or even exclusively a dimension of women's spirituality and therefore restricted to the private realm. As Rosemary Ruether says, women are expected to embrace self-sacrifice or *agape* as appropriate for the domestic sphere while "men are condemned to spend a major portion of their lives in a public world where Christian values such as *agape* seem to have no place."[13]

Research on the public vocation of women uncovers similar themes. Such research is moving us from simple indictments of self-sacrifice in women and calls for female self-assertion, to an analysis of the reasons for difficulty in this realm. In their study, *Other Women's Daughters: Integrative Feminism and Public Spirituality*, Rosemary Curran Barciauskas and Debra Hull conclude that one of the greatest obstacles to integrating love and work is the individualistic ethic that prevails in American society and has divided the women's movement as well.

> In trying to articulate a more inclusive vision that can elicit support from a broad base of individuals we must continue to examine the obstacles which inhibit so many American women and men from either seeing such a vision, or committing themselves to it. Part of the answer may lie in the conflict between altruism and individualism which continues to plague the women's movement, but which has its roots in the larger culture and in the relegating of ethical and spiritual concerns to the private sphere.[14]

What is needed is a new integration of public and private lives, the infusion of values of nurturing and self-giving love into the public sphere and into the working lives of both men and women.

Such considerations are especially important to spiritual direction, since it is often concerned with discerning our Christian calling or vocation to contribute to the redemption of the public sphere. The dilemmas imposed by restrictive understandings of self-sacrifice arise for women in many of their work situations. Women experience ambivalence and conflict as they attempt to balance self-regard and other-regard in a male-oriented workplace which does not pursue or honor such a balance.[15] These dilemmas point to the need for a whole new way of viewing the claims of self and other.

Such a new understanding of the relationship between self and other can be found in an organic world view, one in which all of reality is seen as essentially related. In such a connected world, the movement of anything in the cosmos—rocks or water, plants, animals or human beings—affects all else in some way. Within an organic world view we are not first isolated individuals who later choose to enter into relationships. Rather, the self emerges from relationships; existence is a gift from a previously existing world. Connectedness is prior to freedom and independence. We are literally, as Paul told the Corinthians, one body.

In such a world, interdependence is not an ideal; we cannot escape it. We do not become related when we love one another. We are already related. What love does is redeem the already existing relational web that nurtures our identity. Every act of love strengthens the cosmos; each act of hate weakens it. Denise Levertov points to this truth in her poem, "The Stricken Children."

> And I found the well
> filled to the shallow brim
> with debris of a culture's sickness—
> with bottles, tins, paper, plastic—
> the soiled bandages
> of its aching unconsciousness.[16]

Both water and wells remind us of our interconnectedness and the capacity of those connections to carry grace or destruction. They are symbols of the interdependence of all of life, and the potential consequences of ignoring this truth.

INCLUSIVE COMMUNITY

Either-or thinking is very common in our world. We have a tendency to divide the world in two: light or dark, right or wrong, strong or weak, clean or unclean. This creates a polarized world and exclusive communities. In a polarized society the power to label others according to these dual categories belongs to that segment of society with authority to define things.

Jesus envisioned a different kind of society. In carrying on a conversation with the Samaritan woman, he acts against exclusive community. It is an action in keeping with his message that the reign of God welcomes all persons without exception, a theme played out in various ways in Jesus' message and ministry, for example, in stories of his healings, his encounters with Gentiles, and his interactions with women. His mission embraces all outsiders, not only Samaritans, but Roman centurions and Canaanite women as well. Christian discipleship, the pattern of growth at which spiritual direction aims, involves ever greater appropriation of the inclusive nature of God's reign revealed in Jesus.

A spirituality of exclusion affects both personal and institutional wholeness. It creates thought and language based on us/them categories. We deny what we consider weaknesses in ourselves and project them onto others. Those we define as other—gay or lesbian persons, blacks, women, the poor—are excluded from participation and power. Such a spirituality of denial lies at the heart of racism, sexism, and anti-semitism.

The Spirit calls us from such exclusiveness to all-inclusive attitudes and actions, to a spirituality which refuses to rule out whole areas of human experience and whole groups of human persons. The book of Acts depicts the entire human race—persons of all colors, religions, political and economic systems—as existing, living, and moving within the cosmic womb of the one God (17:24–28).[17] A spirituality of inclusion breaks down categories of "us" and "them" and replaces them with ones that are mutually sympathetic. This spirituality is, as Elisabeth Fiorenza has shown, grounded in Jesus' vision of an inclusive God. It is not a holiness of the elect.

Wholeness spells holiness and holiness manifests itself precisely in human wholeness. Everyday life
must not be measured by the sacred holiness of the
Temple and Torah, but Temple and Torah praxis
must be measured and evaluated by whether or not
they are inclusive of every human being.[18]

As is apparent in the New Testament struggle to break down
barriers between Greek and Jew, slave and free, male and female, such universality requires a gift of the Spirit. Its presence
is also an indication that we are listening to Jesus' Spirit.

Inclusiveness is not merely a human gesture of acceptance; it is an experience of transcendence which discloses a
deeper understanding of God. Love of the outsider leads to a
deeper vision of who God is.

To be touched by the otherness of a hungry African
child, for example, is important not only because it
nurtures a human life, but because it actually transforms one's own inner self and ultimately one's very
vision of who Jesus is and who his Father is.[19]

When we are pulled outward toward transcendence we learn
more of God. A global spirituality, which is another name for
an inclusive spirituality, is therefore not simply a matter of
justice. It is also a call to get rid of idols and worship God in
spirit and truth.

We find God in the otherness of the other. Virginia Mollenkott, in *Godding*, reminds us that God's presence has always appeared to the people in the form of the *other*. When it
was daylight, God was in the darkness of the pillar of cloud.
During the darkness of night, God appears in the brightness of
the pillar of fire. It is then dangerous, she says, for us to reject
what is opposite to what we think ourselves to be, to think
ourselves superior to people who are poorer or richer or darker
than ourselves. In fact, God's presence may be waiting for us
precisely there.[20]

The significance of such an understanding of otherness
was reinforced for me by the experience of a young man in one

of my classes on spirituality. During a guided experience in finding one's symbol or image for the divine, the God-symbol that came to him was a pregnant, native American woman. He was perplexed and troubled by this, but realized it was calling him in some way to move beyond his limited notions of the divine. His struggle symbolizes the way in which the call to inclusiveness is, for all of us, a call to Christian growth.

ELIMINATING OPPRESSION

Water is not only a symbol for God's presence; it is also a symbol of justice. One of the most forceful uses of this imagery is found in the prophet Amos.

> But let justice flow like water, and integrity like an unfailing stream (5:24).

Women's search for a new spirituality is based on a thirst for this justice, justice that is not an intermittent trickle, but a continuous flow. We yearn for the elimination of all interlocking forms of oppression.

Feminist spirituality does not claim that women, in contrast to men, are sinless and in no need of conversion. In fact, we are all called to look at the ways in which we are not only oppressed, but oppressors as well. When women hear the call that God wants them to live fully, it cannot be separated from the call to enable all persons to live fully. Oppression takes varied forms, and involves a double or even triple jeopardy for minority women, older women, and women in poverty. Bell Hooks describes how she experienced marginality in terms of her race as well as her sex.

> To be in the margin is to be part of the whole but outside the main body. As black Americans living in a small Kentucky town, the railroad tracks were a daily reminder of our marginality. Across those tracks were paved streets, stores we could not enter, restaurants we could not eat in, and people we could not look di-

45

rectly in the face. Across those tracks was a world we could work in as maids, as janitors, as prostitutes, as long as it was in a service capacity. We could enter that world but we could not live there. We had always to return to the margin, to cross the tracks, to shacks and abandoned houses on the edge of town.[21]

As Hooks points out, not all women experience oppression in the same way. In the early stages of the contemporary women's liberation movement, she says, some white middle class women argued that motherhood was an obstacle to women's liberation. Many black women, she believes, would have placed racism, availability of jobs, and lack of skills or education at the top of the list of serious obstacles to our freedom as women, but not motherhood. Black women would not have said motherhood prevented them from entering the world of paid work, because they have always worked. Historically, black women have seen work in the home as humanizing labor that affirmed their identity as women; it stood in contrast with labor outside the home which was most often degrading and dehumanizing.[22] Similar differences are found in the way oppression is experienced in women of other cultural, economic, and age groups. Spiritual guidance must be based on recognition of the complex and varied patterns of oppression in women's lives.

In addition, spiritual direction is always linked to a commitment to end injustice, not just for the individual person, but for all persons. Holiness is built on a new politics. It involves a commitment to creating communities of mutuality and justice. The vision of the new person is related to a vision of a new humanity, a new society.

During the weeks in which I was thinking and praying about the implications of the Samaritan woman's story for women's spirituality, I had two dreams. In the first dream I am at a reception of some kind in a large hall. Friends and acquaintances of mine are there, along with people who are complete strangers to me. We are all seated around tables or milling about in groups. The walls of the hall and the table are a drab brown, and I remember being struck by the fact that no flowers or decorations of any kind appear on them. Shortly after the reception begins, five people arrive looking for me. They are all dressed in dark black clothing; the first is a woman, but I cannot distinguish the sex of the others. They take me to a table in a side room, and the woman who is their leader opens a large notebook and tells me that reports have been received of an action of mine the previous summer that is clearly against the rules. They do not say what the action is nor what the rules are, but after informing me that they expect a complete explanation, the leader closes the book and they march out past my friends at the reception. The atmosphere of the dream feels heavy and ominous.

Three nights after this dream of judgment, I had a second dream. In this dream I am seated in a circular chamber that is brightly lit. It is not clear to me whether anyone else is seated around me. My attention is completely focused on the stage which runs around the edge of the chamber on which a style show is taking place; I am looking up at it and smiling. In this style show are women from many nations of the world wearing a wide variety of sacred vestments. They resemble other vestments I have seen, but at the same time they are very different. What I remember of the dream is the vividness of the colors and the diversity of the women and their garments. The women have different skin colors and features. The garments are white but highlighted with golds, deep blues, greens, and shades of rose. They are a variety of lengths and styles. The women are moving freely and joyously, and the garments move with them, as though in a dance. That is all there is to this second dream, my sitting there for some brief moments of this style show, but when I awoke the images were still very vivid for me, as was the feeling of joy and freedom.

These two dreams capture for me the spirit of the Samaritan woman's story. Jesus calls her from the margin to the center of life, from someone judged as unworthy by the tradition, to a role as bearer of revelation to her community. Her story presents an unfinished agenda for all women, but it shows us the path to growth and healing. Spiritual directors are called to be companions and guides as women walk that path.

1. *A World Without Sexism*

Relax yourself and rest peacefully for a time in the presence of God. Then spend some moments letting yourself imagine a world without sexism. What does this world look like? How are people relating to one another and to nature? Do the institutions we now know exist? If so, in what shape? If not, what has replaced them? What is the church like? Take time to envision how those realities most important to you are transformed in such a world.

Now focus on yourself. How are you different in such a world? What qualities do you possess and express? How do you relate to yourself, to others, and to God?

Conclude with prayerful reflection on ways you might live out of this vision even now.

2. *Grounding*

Our spiritual legacy has encouraged us to go beyond our bodies and reach to God in the heavens. On a body level, this has meant pulling energy up into our heads and trying to escape the body. The following exercise fosters a felt bodily connection to the Earth. By letting your energy release down into your torso, hips, legs and feet, you begin to surrender into oneness with God in yourself, your body, the Earth.

Begin standing with your feet parallel, a hip's width apart. If you are with a partner or group of women, do this together holding hands in a circle. Now slowly bend your knees. Look down to see that your knees are tracking over your middle toe, providing clear alignment and support. Now slowly extend your legs without locking or hyper-extending them. Repeat the bend in your knees, this time exhaling through your nose as you let down. Inhale as you lengthen your legs.

This is the basic movement to be repeated for a five to ten minute period. Each time you inhale, fill your belly with breath, and as you exhale, let down into the earth and breathe

48

out any tensions you experience in your body. Close your eyes. With other women, sense the group slowly pulsing up and down together and hear the group breath traveling in and out. Feel the muscles in your feet, legs and hips connecting to our Earth Mother.

"All things connect. What happens to the Earth happens to the children of the Earth"—Unknown Native American.

(This exercise was created by Betsey Beckman, a professional liturgical dancer and movement therapist at the Institute for Transformational Movement in Seattle, Washington.)

3. Women at the Well

Prayer in which we bring into awareness our ties with other women throughout the world helps to strengthen those bonds and increases our resolve to work for the freedom and wholeness of all women.

Either imaginatively or in simple awareness, direct your attention to all those women throughout the world who thirst in any manner, and to the ways in which you are united with them: single mothers who struggle to feed and clothe their children, women at the wells of third world slums, black women in South Africa who live with systemic violence, all those who are in your heart and mind. Let this sense of connectedness come home to you. Be aware that all of you are in God, and God is in you. Listen to their voices.

Then give expression to this thirst by repeating slowly Psalm 42:2 or another prayer of your choice: "My soul thirsts for God, the God of life."

Close your prayer with a passage of promise and hope:

"Whoever drinks the water that I give
will never thirst again.
The water that I give will become a spring within,
welling up to eternal life" (Jn 4:13–14).

49

"The Spirit and the bride say, 'Come!'
Let everyone who listens answer, 'Come!'
Let all those who are thirsty come.
All who want may have the water of life
and have it free" (Rev 22:17).

¹See, for example, the work of Madonna Kolbenschlag in *Kiss Sleeping Beauty Good-Bye* (New York: Doubleday, 1979), and Joann Wolski Conn's helpful analysis in "Women's Spirituality: Restriction and Reconstruction," in *Women's Spirituality*, ed. Conn (New York: Paulist Press, 1986), pp. 9–30.

²(New York: Avon Books, 1972), p. 603. Some commentators view Gertie Nevels herself as the transfiguration of woman into the martyred Christ. See Barbara Hill Rigney, *Lilith's Daughters. Women and Religion in Contemporary Fiction* (Madison: The University of Wisconsin Press, 1982), pp. 13–16.

³(Boston: Beacon Press, 1987), p. 99.

⁴A very helpful summary of some approaches to this issue is Barbara Hilkert Andolsen's "Gender and Sex Roles in Recent Religious Ethics Literature," *Religious Studies Review* 11 (July 1985), 217–23. See also *The Creation of Patriarchy* (New York: Oxford University Press, 1986) in which Gerda Lerner provides a critical historical perspective on the development of patriarchy, a viewpoint many consider natural and normative.

⁵George H. Tavard, *Woman in Christian Tradition* (Notre Dame: University of Notre Dame Press, 1973), pp. 137–138.

⁶"Christian Women and the Struggle for Justice in Central America," in *Speaking of Faith. Global Perspectives on Women, Religion and Social Change*, ed. Diana L. Eck and Devaki Jain (Philadelphia: New Society Publishers, 1987), p. 28. See also *New Eyes for Reading. Biblical and Theological Reflections By Women From the Third World*, ed. John S. Pobee and Bärbel von Vartenberg-Potter (Oak Park, IL: Meyer Stone Books, 1987).

⁷Trans. and ed. E. Allison Peers (New York: Doubleday, 1962), IV, chap. 2, no. 2.

⁸(New York: Simon & Schuster, 1985), p. 44.

⁹A helpful discussion of this can be found in James B. Nelson, *Between Two Gardens. Reflections on Sexuality and Religious Experience* (New York: The Pilgrim Press, 1983), pp. 167ff.

51

[10]*The Politics of Women's Spirituality*, ed. Charlene Spretnak (New York: Doubleday, 1982), p. xviii.

[11](Berkeley: University of California Press, 1985).

[12](Philadelphia: Westminster Press, 1984), p. 33.

[13]Quoted by Barbara Hilkert Andolsen in "Agape in Feminist Ethics," *Journal of Religious Ethics* 9 (Spring 1981), 76.

[14]Unpublished paper, p. 29. The authors are from Wheeling College, Wheeling, West Virginia.

[15]This emerges, for example, in the research reported in Curran and Hull, *Other Women's Daughters.*

[16]*Breathing the Water* (New York: New Directions Publishing Corporation, 1987), p. 33.

[17]See Virginia Ramey Mollenkott's discussion of these verses in *The Divine Feminine. The Biblical Imagery of God as Female* (New York: Crossroad Publishing Co., 1984), pp. 15–16.

[18]*In Memory of Her*, p. 120.

[19]Francis X. Meehan, *A Contemporary Social Spirituality* (Maryknoll: Orbis Books: 1982), p. 16.

[20](New York: Crossroad Publishing Co., 1987), p. 69.

[21]*Feminist Theory: From Margin to Center* (Boston: South End Press, 1984), p. ix.

[22]*Feminist Theory: From Margin to Center*, p. 133.

3

Women Experiencing
and Naming God

We are in the midst of an unprecedented revolution in our language for God. Contemporary challenges to traditional God-language center on its exclusive use of male metaphors, especially that of Father. This one-sided naming of God runs the risk of idolatry, the danger of confusing one human symbol with the divine reality. Furthermore, our limited God-language distorts all our relationships. As Ana-Maria Rizzuto points out in *The Birth of the Living God*, our God-image is a major element in our view of self, others and the world. Its development and influence span the entire life cycle from birth to death.[1]

The exclusive use of male God-language restricts the religious experience of all believers, but it is especially destructive for women. From the time we are very young we learn that all the symbols for what is most sacred in life are male. Ultimate religious authority and meaning are found in a male God, a male savior, and male church leaders. As Carol Christ says, woman "can never have the experience that is freely available to every man and boy in her culture, of having her full sexual identity affirmed as being in the image and likeness of God."[2]

As a consequence, it is difficult for her to believe deeply in her own sacredness, her power, and her capacity to image the divine. No wonder, then, that many women struggle throughout life with feelings of low self-worth.

Spiritual directors are concerned not only with the broader religious and social implications of this ferment, but also with the shape it takes in the lives of individual women. In what ways can spiritual guides support efforts to heal and expand our God-language?

Women enter the current discussion at various levels. Some do not rely on images for their personal prayer, and are most concerned about the liturgical and political force of God-language. Some women are content to retain the traditional images and experience no problem with them. Others find themselves with a broken symbol system, surrounded by traditional images which no longer speak to them. Many of these women are engaged in the journey to new metaphors, attempting to heal old images or integrate new ones into their spirituality.

Keeping in mind these diverse responses to the current crisis in God-language, the spiritual direction context can be helpful in several ways. It can provide a woman with (1) an opportunity to understand and express her own experience of God, (2) an interpretive framework for dealing with the loss of traditional symbol systems, and (3) suggestions for transforming the imagination in relation to our images of God.

EXPERIENCING GOD

Language and experience are interrelated. One aspect of this relationship is the capacity of language to control and limit our experience. This is particularly true of the language of the imagination. Sandra Schneiders makes this point very well in *Women and the Word*. It can easily be established, Schneiders believes, that the God of Judaeo-Christian revelation is not male and that Jesus' maleness is theologically irrelevant.

> This helps very little, however, because the real problem is not in the area of systematic theology but in the area of religious experience or spirituality. How women experience themselves in relation to God, Christ, and Church is profoundly affected by the imputed masculinity of God which is operative in the imaginations of both male and female believers.[3]

We all know persons who find it hard to believe in God's love and mercy because their dominant image of God, usually formed in childhood, is that of an exacting Judge. Likewise, those who relate to God only as Father, King, and Lord have closed out experiences of self and God that might be facilitated by images of God as Mother, Gentle Wind, or Woman in Childbirth. The effort to change language is not an expendable agenda; it has far-reaching consequences for the spiritual life.

Because of the reciprocal relationship between language and experience, religious experience is not only conditioned by, but also shapes, our language for the divine. A variety of approaches to expanding our language for God is then essential. The first, and most revolutionary, is a deepening of our lives of contemplation. Women throughout history have believed in the authority of their own direct experience of God. When that religious experience has been heard, they have enriched our common language for God. Teresa of Avila speaks of the soul as a beautiful palace with walls of crystal; God is a brilliant diamond at the very heart of this palace. From her prayer come images of God as a fountain at the very center of her being or as a brilliant sun giving light to every part of her.

Constance FitzGerald, in an article on impasse and the dark night, formulates well the contemporary significance of this relationship of experience to language.

> Yet every religious experience comes from a meeting with a new and challenging face of God in one's own time and social situation. I suspect that although it is imperative, for example, for feminist theologians to develop new interpretive paradigms that function to

liberate people, only women's *experience* of God can alter or renew our God images and perhaps our doctrine of God.[4]

Contemplative prayer is a way of discovering God, ourselves, and other persons. Continual encounters with God in prayer have power to transform our established images of the divine, whatever they may be.

Contemplation is thus the deepest basis of change and one of the strongest forces both for establishing our identity and for seeing the world in God's light. Through contemplation we prepare for the disclosures of the divine. One woman describes the fruits of her silent prayer of contemplation in this way.

> On some level I am aware of the spirit of life in the body of life. On some level I am aware of my most real self and the most real other at the same time. As I breathe in and out, the inner and the outer, the self and the Other, are somehow not two, but one. I am more and more convinced that we either find our true selves AND God, or we don't find either one, and, of course, only if we have found our true selves and God can we let go of both and let God be God.

In contemplation we can move beyond the rational mode of action, based on the subject/object split which has determined our lives and politics, to a sense of unity with other persons and the environment.

In a variety of ways women are drawing on their experience to influence language for the divine. As previous metaphors prove inadequate to that experience of God, they develop additional images. This process is described in some of their own statements.

> I used to think of God as Father, which was good at the time because my own father was a positive influence on my life. With my more recent understanding of the role of women in the world, I can't image God as male anymore. It's hard for me to image God in any

human form now. I think of God as truth, life, love, energy.

I used to see myself as a child and God as my Father. Now I see myself as an adult in whom God resides. I find God in other people and relate to God through concern for them and for creating a just world—which I view as God's future reign.

I have come to a place where I no longer use words and images in prayer. When I need to use an image to communicate to someone else, I use El Shaddai, the color purple, "the fire and the rose are one."

I see myself as *with* God in whom we live and move and have our being," closer than breathing. It used to be a hierarchy, now it is *cooperation*, being with God. We both moved—God has come "down" and I've gone "up." The Great Dichotomy is dead!

My images of God vary. Sometimes they are from nature—a shelter from the storm; a warm, gentle sun; rain on parched earth. Sometimes God is a pregnant woman, a friend, a male lover.

Primarily I image God as woman, as mother. I also have some familiar images from childhood—God as a tall evergreen tree; God as a Rock; God as the oceanbed without which the ocean would not be ocean; God as Fire. I am especially drawn to John's various "I am . . ." statements. The beating heart is a recent image from the past year or so. So is a clean brightness or radiant light.

I am often sheltered or protected by God. I am hugged or held, loved. Recently I often stand or move forward with God behind me, around me as a cloak. The picture of the child in the hand of God conveys the feeling but that is *not* the image. I do not often now see myself as a child.

Reflected in these women's statements is the theological truth that since God is present in all of creation, any aspect of that creation can be a sacrament of the divine presence. Many images disclose aspects of the divine; none can encompass it. As these women also indicate, changes in our personal images for God occur gradually over a period of time. We may not notice them at first. Spiritual direction is often an opportunity to recognize and appropriate them.

The primary role of a spiritual friend then, in this time of changing language for God, is to support a woman's efforts to grow in a life of prayer and to name God out of that experience. In addition, spiritual direction can be a helpful setting for exploring more fully our images of God and the role they play in our perception of self and world.

No image functions in exactly the same way for every individual. Some women comment in spiritual direction, for example, that they understand theoretically the way in which the image of God as Father has sustained a patriarchal church and culture. However, for them personally, the metaphor has not had patriarchal connotations. As one woman said:

I have never thought of God as father in a stern, judgmental way. Nor in terms of hierarchy. I think I attribute to him the best of the qualities I found in my own father: gentleness, a love of nature, affection and warmth. I can't pray to God as Mother. That image just doesn't speak to me at all.

Another woman, whose father died when she was very young, likewise found that her deepest prayer experiences were with God as Father. She was somewhat apologetic about saying this, because she felt it contradicted the feminist stance she held toward life in other areas. But as she described her prayer, it was clear that in centering herself in prayer to God as Father she experienced love, healing, and an empowering presence that enabled her to move out toward life with courage and energy. As we noted earlier, metaphors for God both shape and are shaped by our life experiences, especially our most significant relationships. Because of their positive experiences of fatherhood or the healing way they have related to God as Father in prayer, this image is for some women free from patriarchal overtones, and functions rather as one appropriate way of experiencing God.

Spiritual classics provide additional examples of the way God-images affect a woman's view of reality. Julian of Norwich wrote a short version of her *Revelations of Divine Love* which she later expanded over a period of twenty years into the Long Text. The Long Text contains not only greatly expanded images of God as female, but a marked decrease in disparaging comments about herself. As her image of God expanded, her self-concept became stronger and more secure.[5]

As is clear from these examples, a spiritual guide's role is not to promote any one image of God, but rather to support a woman's process of understanding how she images the divine and how her images affect her life.

Strong support for this approach comes from the research into the spirituality of the high middle ages by Caroline Walker Bynum. In her *Jesus As Mother*, she examines the writings of women mystics of the thirteenth century, exploring the function of religious imagery in their lives. Setting aside assumptions and unwarranted generalizations, Bynum begins with the religious images of the period and then moves back into the experience of the individuals or groups that produced them. Her research leads her to the conclusion that there is no necessary affinity between thirteenth century women and female imagery.

> If women are particularly attracted by images of women, why is it that monks refer more frequently to the virgin Mary, while women concentrate especially on the infant or adolescent Christ? Clearly other answers are needed.[6]

The same method enables her to understand the relationship between the mysticism of thirteenth century women and their exercise of an authority not grounded in office. It was their mystical union, Bynum finds, which empowered them to serve as counselors, mediators, and channels to the sacraments.

> The visions of the nuns of Helfta projected them into the priestly role from which they were clearly by canon law excluded. Despite an increasing effort in the thirteenth century to curtail clerical activities by women and a clear understanding in theology of women's inferiority in the natural order, these women did not perceive their gender either as a disqualification for service or as an image to express the soul's incapacity or baseness. Their teaching, counseling, and consoling was done with power and serenity.[7]

Bynum's careful reflection on the religious imagery of these women reveals how their religious experience made them question the typical ways religious power was exercised in their time.

Bynum's method underscores some important points about exploring God-imagery in the spiritual direction context: (1) the need to set aside assumptions and generalizations in order to understand more fully the complex role religious imagery actually plays in a person's life, and (2) the importance of noticing the significance religious imagery has for a woman's sense of the authority of the self. Images of God and self are very closely connected, and a change in one brings about a change in the other.

This is borne out by testimony from contemporary women who state that a new awareness of their own authority followed upon changes in their image of God. Rather than being an external force, God became the source of a new inner power.

> Now my sense of God is not outside of myself but a very deep "core" sense of being in God and God being deeply in me. I have a stronger sense of being myself

and having choices. I see myself as strong; before I relied on God to tell me everything. God, I think, is pleased with me and my becoming of age.

God is a deep inner presence in my being and present in others and all of creation. My image is more of one who permeates the human spirit with goodness, which contrasts to a Father-image I once had. Now my relationship with God is very bonded, connected to the core of my being, whole and affirming. It has changed from an up-down relationship, when I imaged God as Father.

I see God as connecting people together—no face or form. I used to be apathetic. I went through the motions but had no real feeling about God or Jesus. He seemed a wimp the way I was educated. Mary was the only one we were comfortable praying to as kids. Then when I began to see how messed up the world was I was *angry.* I had to begin to see God as not all powerful or in control before we could have a relationship. Now I try to see what I can do to help make the world a little better. God doesn't do it alone. God needs our help.

These women experience God as closer and more immanent, but less easily imaginable; this immanence of God is for them the basis of a belief in the interrelatedness of all of life.

Spiritual direction is an opportunity, then, for a woman to give voice to her experience of God and to discover its importance in shaping her understanding of self and the world. While engaged in this process some women find that they have let go of previous images, but that no new symbols have arisen to replace those of a dying patriarchal order. They look to spiritual direction for help in accepting this loss and bringing something new to birth.

INTERPRETING THE LOSS OF SYMBOLS

When familiar religious symbols no longer hold meaning for us, it is important to remember that our spiritual lives take two interrelated paths to God. One path, traditionally called the kataphatic and exemplified by spiritual writers such as Teresa of Avila and Ignatius of Loyola, emphasizes our capacity to reach God through creatures, images, and symbols. It underscores the similarity between God and creation which is the basis for an incarnational and sacramental vision. Annie Dillard's opening statement in *Holy the Firm* conveys something of this vision.

> Every day is a god, each day is a god, and holiness holds forth in time. I worship each god, I praise each day splintered down, splintered down and wrapped in time like a husk, a husk of many colors spreading, at dawn fast over the mountains split.[8]

This kataphatic way has been the dominant approach in western spirituality, and is the spiritual path many women follow.

Today there is a revival of interest in another dimension of the tradition, that approach which sees all particular expressions of God as radically inadequate. The current questioning of patriarchal God-language is one of the forces contributing to renewed awareness of this avenue to God. This path, which is called the apophatic, finds expression in the writings of *The Cloud of Unknowing*, John of the Cross, Simone Weil, and Thomas Merton. It emphasizes that God is "not this, not that." Because of the radical difference between God and creatures, God is best known in obscure awareness, and, at times, in darkness. Meister Eckhart in the thirteenth century spoke with the frequently paradoxical language of this path when he said that it is possible to be so poor that one does not even have a God. The apophatic focus is also captured in the familiar Zen saying that we are not to confuse the pointing finger with the moon to which it points. Everything is a finger pointing to God, but no created thing is God. The "negative way" is not a uniform phenomenon; rather, it is expressed distinctively in different traditions.

These two paths, the kataphatic and apophatic, intersect and converge in most spiritual lives. However, the apophatic tradition provides a helpful interpretive framework for women when traditional God symbols lose meaning for them. This approach stresses God's radical transcendence of social structure and provides a prophetic witness against systems that absolutize assertions about the divine.

The apophatic path goes by way of the desert, with its experience of waiting and struggle, of emptiness and seeming loss of faith. Along this path we may encounter the Dark Night which John of the Cross speaks of as part of the movement from meditation to silent imageless contemplation. Those called to apophatic prayer experience what John of the Cross referred to as a "binding" of their ordinary mental faculties in prayer. The call to this prayer is then really no longer a choice; it becomes the only way left to pray.[9] One woman describes her experience of it in a moving way.

> It was only after the sense of Presence left me that I recognized its existence and importance in my life. Of course I thought the sense of presence left me because I had done something wrong. It never occurred to me that I was embarking on a new stage of my inner life; rather it seemed that my inner life was now over, that perhaps it had been a delusion in the first place. I only knew that I was in pain, that I could not pray in my usual way (or any way at all), that reading scripture was dry and repulsive to me, and that it was painful to go to Mass and the sacraments.

This description conveys well the experience of the apophatic path as a desert where we feel abandoned by God and left to our own resources, cut off from the divine presence that was once our deepest satisfaction and fulfillment.

For a number of women today the desert experience coincides with their increasing inability to relate to the traditional religious symbols that are embedded in patriarchy. As one woman said,

> The old answers that used to speak, no longer speak to me, and the passages of scripture in which I once felt comfort are no longer comforting. There is a silence in me that as yet has no voice.

Some women find help at this time by being introduced to a form of centering prayer, if this has not already been a part of their prayer experience. In such prayer we contact the God who dwells in the depths of our selves, at the center of our existence. Thomas Merton describes this way of prayer as

> a kind of praise rising up out of the center of Nothingness and Silence. . . . It is not "thinking about" anything, but a direct seeking of the Face of the Invisible.[10]

Since it is centered on attention in faith to the presence of God and on resting in God's love, this prayer does not depend on imagining or conceiving an image of God. Women can pray in this way even when all the symbol systems on which they relied are collapsing.

Some women relate to the writings of the twentieth century philosopher and mystic, Simone Weil, when they find themselves in this desert. Simone Weil speaks of prayer as waiting for God or attention. This is a receptive mode of being which creates a space for God's coming. It is an emptiness, but one marked by desire. In illustrating the meaning of attention, Weil recounts an Eskimo story about the origin of light: "In the eternal darkness, the crow, unable to find any food, longed for light, and the earth was illumined."[11] Attention, or desire directed toward God, can open one to the gift of a direct experience of God. Like others who follow the apophatic path, Weil's writings are filled with the language of paradox and contradiction. God is in the absence; with the death of familiar symbols we are thrown back on the experience of God, on watching and waiting for God's coming.

64

Although experiences of darkness deepen awareness of the incomprehensibility of God, they are a painful time. Spiritual friends can provide reassurance that God is present in the darkness, that it is a process of transformation and grace. John of the Cross calls this night of faith the second night; in the movement toward union with God faith becomes the sole guide. Such faith leads us into mystery because it "informs us of matters we have never seen or known, either in themselves or in their likeness."[12] When concepts and images are empty, God is bringing about a transformation in love of our capacity for union. A new experience of God is breaking through as everything is relocated within a new horizon in which it will be radically reinterpreted.

TRANSFORMING THE RELIGIOUS IMAGINATION

The imagination is changed and healed when addressed in its own language, that is, in the concrete language of image, metaphor and story. Integrating a new image into prayer is a different process from analyzing its adequacy from a theological perspective, though the two are related. Myths, symbols, and images touch the deepest levels of the self and affect behavior in ways we may not be totally aware of on a conscious level. New information, though helpful, is not enough. A woman came to spiritual direction after hearing a lecture on images of God. The speaker's points resonated with her experience; she realized that she wanted to expand her God-images. "However," she said, "just saying the words doesn't necessarily make it happen." Another woman wanted to change her image of God as Father. She needed to retain the metaphor in some form in order to heal her relationship with her own father. However, she wanted a new experience of God as Father, and asked if I thought that was possible.

The process of integrating new images into our spiritual lives involves not only *talking* about new metaphors, but praying to God under these new names, seeing self and world through these images, and incorporating them into our litanies and rituals. One woman, for example, who felt strongly attracted to female images for God, began using the passage from Matthew 23:37 for her prayer: "O Jerusalem, Jerusalem, you kill the prophets and stone those who are sent to you! How often have I wanted to gather your children as a mother bird gathers her young under her wings, and you would not!" While praying with this passage, the woman had a very strong experience of the presence of God surrounding her. She came back to this image of Jesus as Mother Hen frequently in her prayer, and moved from it to the image of God as Mother Eagle (Ex 19:4). She said that birds had always been a special part of nature for her, and this might be one reason why she liked these images so much. During the spring she took morning walks around a lake, praying with the image as she saw various birds in the area. It opened to her new dimensions of God's desire for her to be free and strong.

As this woman's case illustrates, a symbol or image achieves power in the spiritual life by gradually unfolding its significance; since the imagination works by association, one symbol often unites with another in expanding and deepening its meaning. As new images are integrated into one's spiritual life, old images are changed in light of them, for example, if God is prayed to as mother as well as father, then the fatherhood of God often takes on new qualities, such as tenderness and nurturance.

As is clear from the previous illustration, the imagination calls for participation. Integration of an image into the spiritual life does not happen if we remain outside observers, studying the metaphor from a detached distance. We must interact with the symbol in some way, establishing a relationship with God through the symbol, and drawing out its meaning in terms of that relationship.

Artistic forms can be helpful here. Because the language of the imagination works by suggestion, its insights are often stated best in indirect ways. For example, we are rediscovering the stream of tradition which names God Lady Wisdom. Lady Wisdom or Sophia offers women a model of divine female power, an image full of strong, creative energy.[13] One way of exploring that power is for women to express in clay the feelings evoked by calling God Lady Wisdom. The use of clay brings out unexpressed feelings one has in relation to an image of God.

Poetry is another avenue of entry into an image. Women who are mothers are frequently drawn to the image of God as mother, not as a parent in relation to themselves, but as an affirmation of the sacredness of their role as mother. Their relationship to the metaphor is one of identification. During a reflection period in a class I taught on female images of God, one mother wandered out to the library steps where she saw another mother nursing her baby. She composed the following piece, which she later shared with the class.

> God is like an Asian mother
> nursing her tiny dark baby
> in the shade on the north side
> of the library, sitting on the ground.
>
> She doesn't speak English
> It doesn't matter.
> I am a nursing mother
> We are one.
>
> She is not ashamed of nurturing
> I need nurturing and
> I am also one who nurtures others.
>
> Blessed be the Name of God.

Exercises in guided imagination are helpful to some women as they attempt to rework images of God, self, and others in light of their new understandings. In her journal one woman recorded part of such an experience.

> Then in inviting my image of God as She to be present,
>   it became very difficult:
>
> She was behind me . . .
> She seemed small . . .
> She would not come forward . . .

> She kept her head down . . .
> She would not speak . . .

I asked her, again, to come to me, but she couldn't.

The woman found this experience to be a very important revelation. She had looked for God in images of sky, rock, and storm, but she saw that God was to be found in the small voice within, though it was still bound and hesitant. She therefore embarked on a prayer of waiting, listening to and nurturing that voice.

This emphasis on approaches to healing the imagination is not meant to obscure the importance of theological reflection. *Thinking* about God in new ways is intrinsic to the transformation of God-metaphors. It is especially important for women whose approach to the spiritual life is primarily through reason. A very helpful instance of such an approach is Sallie McFague's discussion of God as mother, lover and friend in *Models of God.*[14] McFague argues convincingly, for example, that friendship is a rich and hopeful way of speaking about the God-world relationship. The metaphor of friendship conveys certain aspects of a mature relationship with God, such as mutuality and companionship; it expresses the ideal of interdependence among peoples of all ages, both sexes, and whatever color and religion. Furthermore, friendship with God in our ecological and nuclear age can be seen as focused on a common project: the well-being of the earth. Like the models of mother and lover, the model of God as friend reveals a non-hierarchical, inclusive love of all. A theological analysis such as McFague's serves an important function in a woman's spiritual life, clarifying the meaning of God-metaphors and motivating her to expand her relationship to God and to others.

In this chapter we have explored several ways in which the spiritual direction context can help women in a time of changing language for God. Primary among these is support for women's efforts to deepen their lives of contemplation and give expression to the relationship they experience there. Spiritual friendship also supports women in the experiences of darkness and emptiness that result from the loss of familiar symbols.

Finally, it can be a setting for integrating new images into the spiritual life, thus freeing the imagination from the limitations of a language dominated by male images and opening up new possibilities for the spiritual life.

FOR PRAYER AND REFLECTION

1. The Many Names of God

This exercise is a way to enter into the Presence of God through the many names of God which reveal some aspect of the divine mystery. Its purpose is to deepen and widen our experience of God, and free us from constricting images. The list is drawn from the experience of women, biblical passages, and women's mystical literature. It can be expanded from the same sources.

Relax and quiet yourself in some way. Then slowly address God with the following names, entering into the Presence they evoke. If that Presence becomes especially strong with any name, simply rest in it, returning to it when your mind begins to wander.

> You are Fire.
> You are Shelter in the Storm.
> You are Breath.
> You are Wisdom.
> You are Darkness.
> You are Friend.
> You are Lover.
> You are Mother.
> You are Body.
> You are Energy.

2. Praying with New Biblical Images

Here are two biblical images of God as woman, each followed by a brief reflection. Look them over, and then follow the directions at the end.

69

a. *God as a Woman Giving Birth*

"For a long time I have held my peace, I have kept still and restrained myself; now I cry out like a woman in labor, I gasp and pant." (Is 42:14)

Reflections on this symbol: Like a woman in childbirth, God agonizes over our failure to bring about justice, over all the oppression and suffering in our world. God is in travail to bring about a new world.

b. *God as a Woman Searching for What Is Lost*

"What woman, if she has ten silver pieces and loses one, does not light a lamp and sweep out the house and search thoroughly until she has found it? And when she finds it, she calls together her friends and neighbors to say, 'Rejoice with me! I have found the silver piece I lost.' In the same way, I tell you, there is rejoicing among the angels of God over one repentant sinner." (Lk 15:8–10)

Reflections on this symbol: God is like a woman seeker of the lost, deeply concerned about all the alienations we experience. God is with us as we search for ways to heal our broken relations with our bodies, other people, and nature.

Choose one of the biblical images above, or another biblical image which interests you more. Then follow these steps:

(a) Pause to listen to what the symbol says to you.

(b) Address God through this symbol.
   What do you say?
   How do you feel in speaking to God in terms of this symbol?

(c) Then become this symbol and speak to yourself.

When you are finished, close with whatever prayers arise in you.

3. Centering Prayer

   This is one formulation of it:

a. Sit relaxed and quiet.
b. Be in faith and love to God who dwells in the center of your being.

c. Take up a love word and let it be gently present, supporting your being to God in faith-filled love.

d. Whenever you become *aware* of anything else, simply, gently return to the Lord with the use of your prayer word.

e. Let a favorite prayer pray itself.

(This formulation is adapted from: M. Basil Pennington, "Centering Prayer," *America*, February 28, 1987, pp. 169–183).

4. A Ritual of Wholeness: God as Earth, Air, Fire and Water

The ancient elements of earth, air, fire and water convey wholeness and connection with the universe. They are also biblical symbols for God. Women have been closely associated with earth and water. Meditation on these symbols is a way of affirming that women are created in the divine image and of seeing their connection with nature as sacred and life-giving.

This ritual may be done with children or a whole family. Symbols of earth (a plant), air (incense), and water can be added to the use of fire (candles).

Prepare a circle of candles, one facing each of the four directions. Light each candle as you read the scripture passages. Spend some moments in quiet contemplation after each reading.

Begin with a simple prayer that calls on God's Presence in the whole universe. All things are holy; we enter this circle of holiness, the divine milieu.

a. *Lighting Candle to the East: God as Wind*

"God says this: Come from the four winds; come, O breath. Breathe upon these dead that they may live again! I prophesied as God had commanded, and the breath entered into them. They came to life again and stood up on their feet, a great, an immense crowd." (Ez 37:9–10)

Prayer: God of the winds, breathe into us your love.

b. *Lighting Candle to the South: God as Fire*

"God went before them, by day in the form of a pillar of cloud to show them the way, and by night in the form of a pillar of fire to give them light: thus they

71

could travel both day and night. The pillar of cloud never failed to go before the people during the day, nor the pillar of fire during the night." (Ex 13:21–22)

Prayer: God of fire, be in us as life-giving energy and passion.

c. *Lighting Candle to the West: God as Water*

"For I will pour out water on the thirsty land, streams on the dry ground.
I will pour my spirit on your descendants, my blessing on your children.
They shall grow like grass where there is plenty of water, like poplars by flowing streams." (Is 44:3–4)

Prayer: O God, may your waters refresh and renew us.

d. *Lighting Candle to the North: God as Earth*

"You were unmindful of the Rock who bore you. You forgot the God who gave you birth." (Deut 32:18)

Prayer: Give us new life, O God, and make us fruitful in turn. Ground us in you, O God.

Now slowly extinguish each candle.

5. The God Tree: Exploring Your Relationship with God

- Begin by relaxing. Then imagine yourself in summer, somewhere out-of-doors. It might be a place familiar to you, or it might not. But the weather is pleasant . . . you are alone . . . you like being there and alone. Find yourself in a pleasant, outdoor place in summer.

- As you are enjoying being alone out-of-doors, you begin to realize something. So, gently, you become aware that God is appearing to you as a tree. The tree is God. Let that tree slowly come into focus for you.

- What kind of tree is your God tree?
- How does it look?
- Perhaps something is going on around it. If there is, what is happening around your God tree?
- As you are noticing your God tree, you slowly and gently become aware that you are a tree. What kind of tree are you?
- Let it come to you, let it come into focus.

- What is your tree like?
- Where is it in relation to the God tree?
- Perhaps something is going on in or near your tree. If so, what is happening around your tree?
- Are there any other trees near you or the God tree? Are there any other trees in sight? (Maybe yes, maybe no.) If so, what are they like?
- Is anything happening near them?

When you feel finished, slowly come back to your room and time.

(This exercise is adapted from Marlene Halpin, *Imagine That! Using Phantasy in Spiritual Direction*, Dubuque, IA: Wm. C. Brown Company, 1982, pp. 63–64.)

NOTES

[1](University of Chicago Press, 1979).

[2]"Why Women Need the Goddess: Phenomenological, Psychological, and Political Reflections," in *Womanspirit Rising*, p. 275.

[3](New York: Paulist Press, 1986), pp. 6–7.

[4]"Impasse and Dark Night," in *Women's Spirituality. Resources For Christian Development*, p. 302.

[5]See Virginia Mollenkott, *The Divine Feminine*, p. 117.

[6](Berkeley: University of California Press, 1982), p. 173.

[7]*Jesus As Mother*, p. 227.

[8](New York: Harper & Row, 1977), p. 11.

[9]A helpful description of this path is found in Julia Gatta, *Three Spiritual Directors for Our Time: Julian of Norwich, The Cloud of Unknowing, Walter Hilton* (Cambridge, MA: Cowley Publications, 1986), pp. 91–124.

[10]Quoted by M. Basil Pennington, in "Centering Prayer," *America* (February 28, 1987), 169.

[11]*Waiting for God* (New York: Harper & Row, 1973), p. 107.

[12]*The Collected Works of St. John of the Cross*, trans. Kieran Kavanaugh and Otilio Rodriguez (Washington, DC: Institute of Carmelite Studies, 1973), *Ascent of Mount Carmel*, Book II, chap. 3, no. 1.

[13]See Susan Cady, Marian Ronan, and Hal Taussig, *Sophia: The Future of Feminist Spirituality* (New York: Harper & Row, 1986).

[14](Philadelphia: Fortress Press, 1987). See also her *Metaphorical Theology: Models of God in Religious Language*, (Philadelphia: Fortress Press, 1982).

4

Jesus and Women

Carlene, a Roman Catholic who has been very active in her church for many years, was talking recently in spiritual direction about a frustrating conversation she had experienced on the topic of women's ordination. After a special Mass at a neighboring parish Carlene was asked how she had liked it. She replied that the absence of women as leaders of the service had been very offensive to her, that the all-male presence in the sanctuary seemed contrary to the attitude of Jesus toward women. The priest and parishioners talking with her were uncomfortable with this remark, and one of the women responded: "We women have plenty to do. Besides, Jesus did not choose a woman to be one of his twelve apostles." Carlene was preparing to respond to this familiar argument when the conversation was interrupted. She drove home mentally rehearsing various extensions of the conversation and defending herself and her comment. As she did this she found herself turning for support to the story of Mary Magdalene. "Her story is an anchor for my faith," she said. "I keep coming back to the fact that she was the first person to receive a resurrection appearance, that she was called to become an apostle to the apostles. I have a deep conviction that the present treatment of women does not reflect the mind of Jesus. Mary Magdalene's story of faithful discipleship gives me courage, and I resolve again that I will not give up."

Carlene's story illustrates the way women are attempting to free Jesus and his message from the distortions of sexism. The person and message of Jesus are central to Christian spirituality. In the past this could simply be taken for granted in spiritual direction with women. However it presents a special challenge today as women become aware of the way in which Jesus' maleness has been used against them. Although women are redeemed, it is argued, they cannot fully image Christ. The maleness of Jesus is used to support women's exclusion from full participation in the church and from the priesthood.

God became incarnate in a man, not a woman. Christian women wrestle with the many spiritual issues that arise from this fact. Does it mean that a man more adequately expresses God? Does Jesus' naming of God as Father force patriarchy upon us? Do images of Jesus as suffering servant encourage women to endure oppression and suffering as silent victims? Can women identify with a masculine reading of the meaning of redemption? In sum, as some theologians have asked, "Can a male savior really save women?

Theologians are developing helpful insights on these questions, fresh perspectives not just for women but for all Christians. However the heart of the struggle goes on not primarily in theological discussions, but in the actual lives of women. Spiritual direction can support women as they search for a liberating relationship to Jesus and his message. That search involves several facets of a woman's spirituality: (1) how she images her personal relationship with Jesus; (2) how she understands the meaning of Christian discipleship; (3) how she interprets Jesus' teachings. We will look briefly at each of these areas.

RELATING PERSONALLY TO JESUS

Being a Christian involves more than abstract speculation about the meaning of Jesus. It includes a concrete relationship. Spiritual guidance helps us clarify what that relationship is

and what we want it to be. As women explore their own identity and sexuality, shifts occur in the way they image their
relationship to Jesus. This process leads to a critical appropriation of images for Jesus, especially in the case of women who
are looking for female symbols of the divine to ground a sense
of their own sacredness.

One significant difference in the way women and men relate to Jesus is that women cannot experience same-sex identification with the male Jesus of Nazareth in the way men
can.[1] Women relate to Jesus instead in terms of images that are
contra-sexual or applicable to both sexes. They may not be
aware of the way they image Jesus, or the messages they receive from these images. As they clarify what that message is,
women sometimes speak of Jesus as brother or lover, and frequently image their relationship to him as that of friend or
companion, as does this woman.

> Jesus is my friend and mentor. I still see God as an au-
> thority, but not as remote as before. Because of Jesus,
> I can personalize and believe God is for me in my life.

A young woman for whom dance is an important form of
prayer also describes Jesus as companion.

> Recently I danced and found myself in my imagina-
> tion with my sisters and brothers in El Salvador. A
> young man was killed in front of me. I held him and
> wiped the blood from his face. I looked around to see
> who would understand my deep sorrow for this peo-
> ple and this man. I found that out of all that sur-
> rounded me, one friend's eyes were the eyes that
> understood how to be my companion. I looked to Je-
> sus' eyes; they were a companion's eyes as this
> friend's were.

The names women choose for Jesus reveal central elements of
his place in their spirituality.

In addition to the personal metaphors of friend and companion, women find that the "I am" statements in John's gos-

pel encompass important dimensions of their experience of Jesus. These images of resurrection, life, wine, water, bread, light, truth, way, vine, door, and word designate Jesus himself and at the same time describe his gifts. As universal symbols for the life-giving divine powers, they are not tied to Jesus' maleness. They also reflect a connectedness with the earth and with all of life, thereby reinforcing an inclusive vision and the sacredness of the natural world. For all these reasons, they help women enter into a relationship with Jesus.

Women mystics have extended this list of titles for Christ, and their writings can be a source of alternate ways of encountering Christ for women. In a prayer of the thirteenth century mystic, Gertrude of Helfta, we find a wide range of images. She refers to Christ not only as guardian and friend, but as counselor, teacher, lover and the "gem of humanity's nobility."[2] The fourteenth century mystic Julian of Norwich extends this religious imagery to include the title of Mother Christ.

> And our saviour is our true Mother, in whom we are endlessly born and out of whom we shall never come.
>
> For in our Mother Christ we profit and increase, and in mercy he reforms and restores us, and by the power of his Passion, his death and his Resurrection he unites us to our substance.[3]

Julian's references to Christ as Mother have been described as androgynous, since they combine both male and female attributes. What the experience of women mystics attests is that it is possible to relate to Jesus in ways that do not glorify male reality at the expense of female experience. Like these mystics women today can exercise great freedom in the use of metaphors to describe their relationship with Jesus.

However, many of these metaphors still leave women searching for greater identification with the central figure of their faith. When she turns to Jesus as pattern or model for human existence, a woman's imagination cannot make an immediate leap from Jesus to self. Understanding why this is so requires an appreciation of how both visual and linguistic im-

78

ages function in a person's spirituality. As Margaret Miles notes in *Image As Insight*, visual images form us by attraction; over time a complex of memories, associations and longings are created in us by the image and provide the basis of its power.[4] What Miles says of visual images is true as well of linguistic images. The image shapes a person's self-image and values.

In relating to Jesus as model, a woman must be able to see how his historically circumscribed life intersects with her experience. It is true that this same movement occurs in the lives of anyone who is not a young Jewish male living in first century Palestine, in other words, the vast majority of Christians. The particularities of Jesus' life do not apply to most of his followers, and Christian discipleship is not meant to be imitation of these culture-bound particulars. The Spirit's role is to link our lives and times with Jesus' life. But in addition to the cultural and racial differences that Christians of later periods must transcend in relating to Jesus' story, women must deal with the gender differences and the traditional use that has been made of these to reinforce woman's oppression.

In their search for identification with Jesus, some women focus their spiritual lives less on a relationship with the historical Jesus of Nazareth and more on the presence of the living Christ in their lives. As Rosemary Ruether expresses it,

> Christ, as redemptive person and Word of God, is not to be encapsulated 'once-for-all' in the historical Jesus. The Christian community continues Christ's identity. As vine and branches Christic personhood continues in our sisters and brothers. In the language of early Christian prophetism, we can encounter Christ *in the form of our sister*.[5]

Jesus of Nazareth in a resurrection body transcends all human limitations, including human maleness. The risen Christ becomes One Body with us all.

Relating to Christ in terms of the body of Christ has always been very fruitful for one's personal life of prayer. This image conveys an experience of presence that leads to identification. It focuses on the meaning of Christianity as participation in a body and therefore affirms the significance of physical existence, of all creation, and of the resurrection of the body. A woman describes her understanding of it this way.

> I find my relationship with God is with Christ, very personal and very nurturing. Jesus has said he lives in us and asks us to live in him.

The symbols of the mystical body and the communion of saints are also important language for connectedness and wholeness. One woman spells this out in relation to the death/resurrection mystery and the eucharist as body of Christ.

> I think specifically of the growing awareness and final understanding that all life is sustained by the death of other living creatures, and sustains new life by its death in turn—that interconnectedness of life and death, all part of a single spiraling continuum, connects the mundane actions of preparing dinner and the transcendent ritual of Christian communion.

Beyond such key religious experiences, there is very little visual imagery that comes to mind, she says, when she thinks of God or Christ: "The Divine Presence no longer can be adequately contained for me in a concrete image."

Although images are never adequate, they are very powerful forces in shaping our relationship with Jesus. Margaret Miles makes this point as she describes the power of visual images in religious worship.

> The image is valued because of its power to move, to focus the sense and the mind, and to offer a mnemonic aid that gathers the worshipper's strongest and most fundamental ideas, emotions, and memories in an enriched present. An image deplored by an art critic or a theologian may nevertheless contain the power to carry the worshipper to the psychic place in which worship occurs.[6]

Theological assertions that the risen Christ transcends the concrete particulars of history do not have the power that a single image has to bring about this emotional healing and focus for worship. Women's imaginations need the deep emotional healing and affirmation that come from seeing the image and likeness of Christ conveyed more fully in relation to them.

In this regard we can learn from the way the art of many cultures and races has expressed the inclusiveness of Christ by giving him diverse faces: black, native American, oriental, African. Such artistic expression conveys the theological truth that the incarnation embraces all of human nature and our human condition, all women and men of every race and social condition. During Holy Week in 1984 the Episcopal Cathedral of St. John the Divine temporarily hung behind its main altar a four-foot bronze figure which portrayed the crucified Christ in female form. The dean of the cathedral dubbed the statue, sculpted by Edwina Sandys, "Christa." The statue drew mixed responses. For some it was a positive religious experience; others found it "theologically and historically indefensible."[7]

Depicting Christ's transcendence of gender through female images evokes more shock and resistance than expressing his transcendence of race and culture. Female Christ images are equally important, however, and no less orthodox theologically. To say that Christ cannot be imaged as a woman is to imply that women cannot, in fact, image Christ. Rosemary Ruether tells of an encounter in a class she was teaching on violence against women. One of the women in the class told of her experience of being raped in a woods, and recounted the fact that during the rape she had become convinced that she would be killed and had resigned herself to her impending death. After the rapist fled, she found herself still alive, and experienced a vision of Christ as a crucified woman. Commenting on this vision which had filled her with relief and healing, she said: "I would not have to explain to a male God that I had been raped. God knew what it was like to be a woman who had been raped."[8]

In addition to visual images, women need stories of Christ figures who are women. Such figures concretize the redeemed humanity which Christ reveals. Christians have always been aware of the need to see the message of Christ embodied by persons of their own culture and historical era. For women, however, this embodiment supplies something missing in the gospels: the incarnation of God in terms of female experience. Spiritual direction is a context where women can be explicit about their search for such figures. If spiritual direction takes place in a group setting, women can share with one another those Christ figures they discover in friendships with women, in their worship and ministry, in the arts and literature, and in their personal prayer lives.

WOMEN AS CHRISTIAN DISCIPLES

One dimension of a personal relationship with Jesus is the living out of his vision. Much of spiritual direction is spent with the concrete questions involved in being followers of Jesus. Following Jesus, or discipleship, is based on a commitment to Jesus' project of a redeemed humanity. Many women are convinced that Jesus believed in and struggled for the things they value. They remain disciples of Jesus in spite of their awareness of the ways in which the institutional church has betrayed Jesus' message regarding women. With the energy of this conviction, women are beginning to formulate a new paradigm for discipleship, one which grounds their creativity and freedom along with that of all persons.

Several gospel themes support a liberating discipleship for women. They flow from Jesus' central message regarding the reign or realm of God. The New Testament does not contain a definition of the reign of God; what we find instead are many models of human relationship through which we glimpse something of the mystery of the reign, stories of rich and poor people, judges and penitents, landlords and tenants. The parables of Jesus, which include female as well as male imagery, call us to bring about God's reign. They can therefore be a fruitful entry into prayer for women.

Theologian Sallie McFague considers the reign of God, not the fatherhood of God, to be the root-metaphor of Christianity.

As such, it is not concerned with divine or human *nature*, but with a new kind of *relationship*.[9] The relationship of father and son is one way of expressing it, but other metaphors will be needed to sustain its complexity and richness: God as mother, friend, liberator, healer. We know this relationship only indirectly; no other kind of relationship can be simply identified with it.

While we cannot totally define God's reign, we know that human liberation is central to it.[10] Jesus speaks of a coming of God which we are to make a present reality here on earth. It will be a time of the vindication of those who are socially and religiously marginal. Jesus' mission to inaugurate God's reign is sounded early in Luke's gospel, as he responds to John's question, "Are you the one who is to come?" Jesus' reply evokes images from Isaiah.

> Go and tell John what you have seen and heard: the blind receive their sight, the lame walk, lepers are cleansed, and the deaf hear, the dead are raised up, the poor have good news preached to them. (Lk 7:22)

Jesus calls us to a new way of being in the world. What this means for the spiritual journey of marginal persons such as women is that God's redeeming action is taking place right now as they seek their own liberation and that of others. Far from supporting the oppression of women, Jesus' vision calls for the elimination of structures of domination and submission. All who call themselves his disciples share this prophetic mission.

The stories of women in the New Testament portray the liberating power of Jesus' presence and message. He expands their horizons and calls them forward. His message of liberation tells women to expect and seek life now, not simply to wait for life after death. It provides a motivation for changing the relationships which oppress them as well as others.

Women have become involved in a variety of ways and at many levels in the struggle for liberation. The impact of such commitment is captured in her "Poem for South African Women" in which June Jordan commemorates the 40,000

women and children who on August 9, 1956, protested apart-
heid in the South African capital. Jordan concludes the poem,
which she presented at the United Nations on August 9, 1978,
with these lines.

> And the babies cease alarm as mothers
> raising arms
> and heart high as the stars so far unseen
> nevertheless hurl into the universe
> a moving force
> irreversible as light years
> traveling to the open
> eye
>
> And who will join this standing up
> and the ones who stood without sweet company
> will sing and sing
> back into the mountains and
> if necessary
> even under the sea
>
> *we are the ones we have been waiting for*[11]

Jesus brings the good news that those who have no voice—the
sick, sinners, foreigners, women—are valued and are called to
full personhood. He clears a way through tradition and law for
the emergence of the full humanity of those he meets. In relating to Jesus as liberator, women are challenged to develop
the fullness of their human possibilities.

In this context the maleness of Jesus is no longer primary.
It may have been historically important because it enabled Jesus to critique the established order from within, as a male and
therefore as a member of the privileged class. But identification with Jesus is based on shared vision rather than on gender.

Along with this message of liberation, the New Testament presents God's reign as an *inclusive* reality. Its basis is
the all-inclusive love of a God who lets the sun shine and the
rain fall equally on the righteous and on sinners (Mt 5:45). As
Elisabeth Fiorenza says:

84

> This God is a God of graciousness and goodness who accepts everyone and brings about justice and well-being for everyone without exception.[12]

The earliest Jesus traditions call this God of gracious goodness divine Sophia or wisdom. Sophia, the God of Jesus, wills the wholeness and humanity of everyone; no one is excluded. Christians, then, are called to the same practice of inclusiveness and equality lived by Jesus, to a discipleship of equals.

Jesus' message of the reign of God thus supports women's efforts to overcome dualisms and work for an inclusive world. As we saw earlier, women want to heal the alienation and division caused by attitudes toward diversity. Rather than separating us from aspects of ourselves and others, differences such as male and female, body and spirit, intuition and reason can become mutually enriching. Jesus attempted to bring about such a reconciliation of opposites.

This line of thinking has influenced the interpretation of that central Christian symbol, the cross. Instead of viewing the cross as a symbol of victimization, theologians such as Patricia Wilson-Kastner see it as the unifier of alienation and painful diversity. In the cross, dualisms are overcome in an act of reconciliation.[13] The crucifixion, Wilson-Kastner believes, witnesses to a truth feminism affirms: dualisms, be they of dominance and submission, male and female, or matter and spirit, have no place in a Christian understanding of a redeemed universe. In a similar vein, Leonardo Boff speaks of the cross as the symbol of reconciliation creating a new humanity. When we participate in this reconciliating focus, we experience the force of the future breaking into our world.[14]

The dream of healing the divisions caused by hierarchy is being fulfilled among us then by the work of the Spirit of the Risen Jesus. Wilson-Kastner sums this up well.

> Power and insignificance, matter and spirit, activity and inertia are united through the resurrection. The life of the risen Christ that pervades all things unites the divided, and continues as an active force for reconciliation in the world. Feminism, with its strong

85

drive both to preserve the integrity of all beings and yet nurture the interconnectedness of the world, is confirmed in the figure of the risen Christ.[15]

Diversity is not lost in this unification; rather differences enrich the unity. Such a vision of redeemed humanity is not new; it is rooted in traditional interpretations of the resurrection. However, combined with contemporary awareness of the way in which dualisms have functioned in oppression, it serves as a vision of redeemed humanity that can ground the discipleship of women.

WOMEN AND JESUS' TEACHINGS

Along with questions regarding their personal relationship with Jesus and their call to discipleship, women also bring to spiritual direction issues related to the application of Jesus' teaching to their lives. It is clear that certain interpretations of Jesus' message have been death-dealing, not life-giving, for women. Some of these teachings, such as love as self-sacrifice, sin as pride and disobedience, and the meaning of forgiveness, are dealt with in other chapters. Here we will look at another influential aspect of that teaching as it has affected women: the meaning of suffering as redemptive.

A major critique of Christianity by feminists is that it leads women to believe it is their place to suffer, blinding them to oppression. This concern was forcefully expressed by Mary Daly in *Beyond God the Father.*

> The qualities that Christianity idealizes, especially for women, are also those of a victim: sacrificial love, passive acceptance of suffering, humility, meekness, etc. Since these are the qualities idealized in Jesus 'who died for our sins', his functioning as a model reinforces the scapegoat syndrome for women.[16]

Such a justification of suffering can lead women to remain silent about sexual abuse, stay in marriages where they are battered, and set aside their own legitimate needs in order to take care of others.

A first step in conversation with women around this issue is ascertaining the meaning the cross and suffering have in their faith lives. The cross, like all symbols, is multivalent. Its meaning for women varies, and changes for an individual woman over the course of a lifetime. The older women I work with in a nursing home setting, because of their experience of multiple losses over which they have no control, relate to the cross in a different way from some of the younger women I see in spiritual direction. But women of all ages bring to spiritual direction experiences with suffering that challenge all they thought they understood regarding it. They come in grief over the death of a family member or friend. As caregivers or as ministers in hospitals they see the impact of disease and suffering in human lives. They know the hunger and pain of peoples of the world, or experience disease and senseless loss in their own lives. I find that they often feel helpless and hopeless in the face of all of this suffering. Depending on their own relationship to the tradition, the religious art to which they have been exposed, and their personal experience of suffering, women may have internalized traditional interpretations of the crucifixion in unhelpful ways.

The following two women illustrate this point. The first relates to the symbol of Christ on the cross in a way that leads her to resignation and passive acceptance of present suffering.

> It also reminds me that all the pains and wounds suffered in life are transient, and that there will be eternal happiness and love with God.

As her comments indicate, the promise of resurrection can function as a validation of suffering, so that one endures pain, humiliation, and violation of one's rights in view of a future reward. In contrast, United Methodist bishop Leontine Kelly sees the cross as part of the passage to liberation.

> In several areas and times of my own life, I have moved out in trepidation and trembling. The joy I

have found in times when I have dared to shed the old
for the new has come from the willingness of sisters
of faith to share the risk with me. The very nature of
risk is uncertainty and great anticipation. It is faith in
the unknown based on trust in a God whose steadfast
love is from everlasting to everlasting and whose revelation of love in the life, death, and Resurrection of
Jesus Christ affirms liberation from any condition of
bondage.[17]

Kelly views the cross as a call to courage for oppressed persons
who struggle for freedom and life, no longer a symbol used by
the powerful to keep others in submission and passivity with
exhortations that they bear the cross.

Clearly an interpretation of the suffering and death of Jesus is of paramount importance in spiritual direction with
women. Growth in the Spirit involves offering women alternate ways of integrating the meaning of the cross into their
lives. As Carolyn Osiek says in *Beyond Anger. On Being a
Feminist in the Church*, the symbol of the cross

needs to be recovered, reclaimed, and reappropriated
in a new context where it will no longer aid the cause
of oppression and passivity, but the cause of free response to the claims of the Gospel. The cross can become for women a symbol not of victimization and
self-hatred, but of creative suffering, actively em-
braced, which transforms and redeems.[18]

For Osiek the cross is a symbol of contradiction. Followers of
Jesus who choose to live out his call to the reign of God as a
discipleship of equals will experience the violent opposition
aroused by this choice. The cross is the price paid by those who
attempt to realize this vision.

Jesus did not glorify suffering. Nor did he choose suffering
and the cross as something intrinsically good. What he did, and
what he asks his disciples to do, is to choose integrity and
faithfulness without being deterred by threats or pain. Carter
Heyward summarizes this well in *The Redemption of God*.

Any theology which is promulgated on an assumption that followers of Jesus, Christians, must welcome pain and death as a sign of faith is constructed upon a faulty hermeneutic of what Jesus was doing and of why he died. This theological masochism is completely devoid of passion. The notion of welcoming, or submitting oneself gladly to, injustice flies in the face of Jesus' own refusal to make concession to unjust relation.[19]

Jesus' death was an unjust act, done by humans who chose to reject his way of life and sought to silence him. In the struggle for liberation, Heyward contends, there will be suffering, but not glorified suffering. The death, suffering, and pain will result from daring to live our lives in immediate love relationships with each other.

A woman's relationship to Jesus is clearly a central issue in spiritual direction. There are many facets to this relationship, and their significance will vary for individual women. However, there are resources for dealing creatively with them as they arise in spiritual direction. Women need not abandon Jesus and the Christian message as they become aware of the impact Jesus' maleness has had on them. That awareness can lead to ways of imaging Jesus, of describing discipleship, and of living out the Christian vision that are compatible with a woman's integrity and growth.

FOR PRAYER AND REFLECTION

1. Who Will Roll Away the Stone? An Exercise in Guided Imagination

Read: Mark 16:1–8

Relax and quiet yourself.

Now imagine that it is very early on a Sunday morning. You are in Jerusalem, not far from the place where Jesus was executed, on your way to his tomb. The sun is just rising. Take in its gentle light as it begins to expand across the sky . . . Notice the lights and shadows that play about at this time of morning. Listen to the sounds of the countryside as it slowly begins to awaken from sleep . . . Smell the spicy aroma of the myrrh and aloes you are carrying with you.

You are in the company of three strong and faithful women. What feelings do you share with one another about the events of the previous days? . . . Enjoy the companionship and support you experience with these women.

As you talk, you express to one another your concern about rolling back the stone from the entrance to the tomb. What does this stone represent to you? . . . Why do you keep on walking even though you are not certain how you will get past this obstacle? . . . What feelings do you share with one another about the stones which block your access to Jesus? . . . Spend some time with these questions and concerns.

As you get close to the tomb you suddenly notice that the stone has already been rolled back. What are you feeling now? . . .

Stoop down now to enter the tomb. A bright light greets you, and you realize that Jesus is not in the tomb, but is risen. What are you feeling? . . .

Still somewhat stunned, you realize that you are expected to carry this news to the other disciples and Peter. What response do you and the other women have to this? . . .

Whatever your response, you now find yourself running with the other women from the tomb. Why are you afraid? . . . What keeps you from speaking the good news you have discovered? . . . Or do you break through this silence? . . . What helps you find a voice to speak the message you have learned from your experience in the empty tomb? . . .

Spend some time with these reflections and any prayers which arise in you. Then, when you are ready, close your meditation.

2. A Meditation on the Presence of Sophia—God

Meditate on the following passages which describe the presence of Sophia-God. At the end of your prayer, draw together in your journal any new insights that come to you.

>*Proverbs 3:18*—Comforting and nourishing.
>*Wisdom 7:24*—Divine creative power in all things.
>*Wisdom 7:27*—The source of newness and growth.
>*Luke 11:49*—Jesus as Sophia.

3. Praying Jesus' "I Am," Sayings

The "I am" sayings in John's gospel can be a fruitful avenue of meditation on Jesus' universal salvation and healing. The following are phrases based on these sayings. Choose one and repeat it slowly, allowing it to center your heart. If you become distracted, simply return to the phrase again.

>Water falling on the rock.
>The seed descending softly.
>Light illumining the world.

You may want to create your own phrases from your favorite "I am" sayings.

4. The Cross in Your Life: A Journal Exercise

a. What does the cross of Jesus symbolize for you? If you can, recall the history this symbol has for you. How was it presented to you as a child? What images do you have of it from art, churches, holy cards? What emotions do you associate with the cross? In what way, if at all, do you identify with Jesus on the cross?

b. How does the meaning of suffering enter into your spirituality? Do you associate suffering with holiness? With God's will? What religious images, stories, and teachings do you call on to help you deal with the suffering that occurs in your life?

c. What would you like to change, if anything, about the way the cross and the meaning of suffering now function in your spiritual life?

[1] Sandra Schneiders clarifies the issues surrounding the maleness of Jesus in *Women and the Word.*

[2] Quoted in Carolyn Bynum, *Jesus As Mother,* p. 188.

[3] *Showings,* trans. Edmund Colledge, O.S.A., and James Walsh, S.J. (New York: Paulist Press, 1978), pp. 292 and 294.

[4] (Boston: Beacon Press, 1985), p. 146. See also *Immaculate and Powerful. The Female in Sacred Image and Social Reality,* ed. Clarissa W. Atkinson, Constance H. Buchanan, and Margaret R. Miles (Boston: Beacon Press, 1985).

[5] *Sexism and God-Talk. Toward a Feminist Theology* (Boston: Beacon Press, 1983), p. 138.

[6] *Image As Insight,* p. 9.

[7] "As sculptor sees female Christ, some see scandal," *Chicago Tribune,* April 25, 1984, section 1, p. 10.

[8] "Feminist Theology in the Academy," in *Christianity and Crisis* 45 (March 4, 1985), 61.

[9] *Metaphorical Theology,* pp. 145ff.

[10] See Rosemary Ruether, *Sexism and God-Talk,* pp. 116–138.

[11] *Voices of Women. Poetry By and About Third World Women* (New York: Women's International Resource Exchange, 1981), p. 37.

[12] *In Memory of Her,* p. 130.

[13] *Faith, Feminism, and the Christ* (Philadelphia: Fortress Press, 1983), pp. 89ff.

[14] *Jesus Christ Liberator. A Critical Christology For Our Time,* trans. Patrick Hughes (Maryknoll, NY: Orbis Books, 1978), pp. 237–38.

[15] *Faith, Feminism, and the Christ,* pp. 114–115.

[16] (Boston: Beacon Press, 1973), p. 77.

[17] "Women: Witnesses to the Resurrection," *Sojourners* 16 (April 1987), 23.

[18] (New York: Paulist Press, 1986), p. 65.

[19] (Lanham, MD: University Press of America, 1982), p. 58.

5

Praying with Scripture

Generations of women have turned to the bible for courage and inspiration, counting on the scriptural word to challenge their faith and grace their lives. But as women become aware of the bible's role in their domination and dehumanization, it becomes increasingly difficult to trust the bible and rely on it for prayer. How can women relate to writings that are the product of a patriarchal culture, writings which function as the final appeal in claims for male superiority and the subordinate role of women? Can the bible still be the Word of God for us? Can we turn to scripture as a resource for prayer?

Although the bible is used to bar woman's entrance to freedom and new life, it is also our heritage and a life-giving resource for many women. The bible has both enslaved and freed women. Hence an important part of spiritual direction is a reappropriation of scripture based on awareness of its oppressive as well as liberating dimensions.

Feminist biblical scholars are showing us the way, as they struggle with issues of interpretation and authority in the bible and shed fresh light on familiar scripture passages.[1] Because of the work of these scholars, women now have several new avenues for praying with scripture: (1) discovering ourselves in the stories of biblical women; (2) finding hope in liberating scripture passages; (3) remembering and mourning women's pain; (4) listening to the bible's silences. After examining these four approaches, we will conclude with some brief reflections on resources for women who find that, in spite of new insights, they cannot pray with scripture at all.

DISCOVERING OURSELVES IN BIBLICAL WOMEN

Praying with scripture is one way to let the stories of biblical women intersect with our own stories. These women then become models for our own survival and growth. In the past we may have overlooked them, failing to notice Miriam in the story of Moses, or Phoebe in the letters of Paul. This is partly because the writers themselves mention these women simply in passing. Often, too, the stories of biblical women were presented only in terms of prevailing patriarchal motifs: Mary of Nazareth as virgin and mother, Mary of Magdala as siren and sinner. As one woman said in reflecting on her relationship with the women in scripture,

> The stories were familiar to me, but I had not recognized the women figures as significant or acknowledged their contributions.

Lifting out the stories of women in the bible can supply us with new sources of religious identity and inspiration.

In preparing for such prayer it is helpful to cultivate two attitudes: openness to hearing what we have not heard before, and willingness to let biblical women speak with their own voices, voices long muffled by the layers of interpretation we may have learned since childhood. Such prayer is founded on suspicion of conventional interpretations. One woman begins her reading of a passage with this prayer.

> O Wisdom, let me see with new eyes so that I may not pass by the women in these passages as women have been passed by, unnoticed, so often before. Open my

94

ears to hear their voices in fresh and perhaps surprising ways. Let the power of their lives become a grace in my own.

Praying the stories of biblical women can take any of the many paths for praying with scripture: meditation or active reflection on a passage, contemplation or receiving the Word in love, imaginative prayer, dance, or journaling.

If women seek help in approaching these stories, the form of contemplative prayer known through the centuries as *lectio divina,* or sacred reading, is an avenue many find fruitful. It is a way of praying by listening, opening ourselves to God and allowing the words of scripture to flow into us to comfort or challenge. Instead of actively trying to puzzle over passages of scripture, we quietly let the words sink in. This prayer involves a three-part process: (1) *Lectio* or reading. We take up a section of scripture and read until a word or sentence attracts us. (2) *Meditatio* or meditation. We stay with that word or sentence for a time, repeating it, savoring it, letting it enter into us. (3) *Oratio* or personal prayer. We speak to God or rest silently in God's presence.

Whatever the form of prayer a woman chooses, the following can serve as helpful starting points for discovering her own story in the stories of biblical women.

1. Stories of Healing

In several gospel scenes we see Jesus as healer, and women as paradigms of strong faith. Notice these themes, for example, in two different stories:

Matthew 15:21828.	The Canaanite woman.
Mark 1:29–31.	Peter's mother-in-law.

In its broadest sense, healing means making whole. These stories therefore raise for us questions such as: How do I want to be healed? Where do I identify with the stories of these women?

Resurrection is an experience of healing, and women are

intimately connected with resurrection and life throughout the gospels, not only in the resurrection narratives. Notice women's relationship to this theme in the following stories:

Mark 5:21–24.   The raising of the daughter of Jairus.
Luke 7:11–17.   The raising of the son of the widow of Nain.
John 11:1–44.   The raising of Lazarus.

2. Stories of Faith, Initiative and Risk-Taking

Women are marginal members of society by the fact of their gender, but often become doubly so if they are a Gentile like the Canaanite woman or ritually unclean like the woman with the hemorrhage. As you read the stories of these women, relate them to areas of your life where you want to show more self-determination and take more risks. How can you imagine yourself acting differently in light of the stories?

Luke 18:1–8.   The widow and the unjust judge.
Matthew 9:20–22. The woman with the hemorrhage.

3. Stories of Women in a Patriarchal World

a. Exodus 1:8–2:10

In your prayer enter into the experience of both the midwives who are wise and courageous in their response to pharaoh in Exodus 1:15–22, and Moses' mother and pharaoh's daughter who defy the pharaoh in Exodus 2:1–10.[2] Notice how the women of Exodus refuse to cooperate with oppression, and how God acts through them to free the chosen people. Through these stories we learn that liberation begins with the courage of women; change can come through small resourceful actions.

b. The Books of Ruth, Esther, and Judith

In her reflections on the three short stories of Ruth, Esther, and Judith, Toni Craven points out that their tales are remarkably similar.[3] They are the only women whose names are titles of biblical books, indicating that the community saw their stories as valid embodiments of the covenant relationship. Craven shows how the plot of each of the books moves from tragedy to triumph through the resolute acts of a woman. But the woman's success does not result from miracles; rather, victory comes because she uses well the human resources at hand. Ruth heeds the advice of her mother-in-law about securing a spouse and home; Esther defeats the enemy by persuading the Persian king to follow her wishes; Judith delivers her community by beheading the enemy general and then leading a military counteroffensive.

These actions take place in a world of male dominance, a world where independence and decision-making belong to men. But, as Craven shows, in this setting Ruth, Esther and Judith emerge as independent women, influencing their covenant communities in unconventional ways. Despite the repugnance women sometimes feel at the beheadings and military contexts of these stories, they find these three women compelling models of faith. The following are questions that can help to deepen prayer and reflection on the stories of Ruth, Esther, or Judith:

How does this woman preserve the faith of her community?

Does she carry out or reject traditional roles for women?

In what ways does she bring about change?

How is faith lost or found in her story?

What qualities of this woman do you admire? Do you feel repulsed by anything in her story? Why?

What links do you find between her story and your own story?

4. The Reign of God in Female Imagery

Jesus uses female as well as male imagery to describe the reign of God. Such metaphors leave room for the listener's imagination as well as for the work of the Spirit. The meaning of the metaphor is finally fulfilled in the imagination of the person actively receiving it. In your prayer, enter into these images of the reign, letting new understandings of God's vision for the world come to you as you turn the metaphor over in your heart:

> Matthew 13:33.   The reign as yeast in flour.
> Luke 8:16–18.   The lamp on a lampstand.

Receive the image in the same way you would listen to a song or read a poem. Try painting the metaphor or dialoguing with it. Let it connect with other images of bread and light in the gospels.

5. Stories of Women Disciples

Another way to identify with women as paradigms of true discipleship is to pray through one gospel, listening to women's stories and noticing how they live out the call to discipleship. Women have found the gospels of Mark and John especially helpful for this.

a. Mark's Gospel

Mark's emphasis on suffering discipleship is well known, but it is especially important for women to notice that this suffering is not an end in itself, but is the result of solidarity with the outcasts of society. In Mark's gospel, women are shown to be true disciples who have left everything and followed him on the way, even to the cross.

> Though the twelve have forsaken Jesus, betrayed and denied him, the women disciples, by contrast, are found under the cross, risking their own lives and safety. That they are well aware of the danger of being arrested and executed as followers of a political insurrectionist crucified by the Romans is indicated in the remark that the women 'were looking from afar.' They are thus characterized as Jesus' true 'relatives.'[4]

In meditating on this gospel, notice especially Mark's account of the women who witness Jesus' death and resurrection (15:40–47; 16:1–8).

b. John's Gospel

John shows women living out Jesus' call to love. They choose life and love over against the hatred and death-dealing powers of the world. Five women disciples stand out in the gospel.

John 2	Mary of Nazareth at Cana
John 4	The Samaritan Woman
John 11	Martha
John 12	Mary of Bethany
John 20	Mary of Magdala

You might journal about the stories of these women, using the following questions as a guide:

How do these women represent the fullness of faith and discipleship?

What is revealed to them?

How do woman's strength and initiative come through in the accounts?

Developing a litany based on the insights you receive into these women's lives is a good way to close your journaling or prayer. It can arise spontaneously from your encounter with their stories, for example,

Martha, courageous friend of Jesus,
witness to the meaning of resurrection:
I give thanks for your life.

If a group of women is reading scripture together, their reflections can be gathered into one litany.

FINDING HOPE IN LIBERATING PASSAGES

Praying with scripture can sustain a vision of a redeemed society. We pray to deepen our dream of a new creation and of universal human liberation. This prayer presupposes a critical approach to biblical texts, recognition of the dual nature of the bible as both enslaver and liberator. We reject approaches which strengthen oppression and contribute to women's lack of freedom, finding the authority of scripture in its support of the full humanity of all persons.[5] Letty Russell enunciates such a view as she describes the bible's role in her life. Evidence for a biblical message of liberation for women and other marginalized groups is not found, Russell believes, only in particular stories about women and female images of God.

> It is found in God's intention for the mending of all creation. The Bible has authority in my life because it makes sense of my experience and speaks to me about the meaning and purpose of my humanity in Jesus Christ. In spite of its ancient and patriarchal world-views, in spite of its inconsistencies and mixed messages, the story of God's love affair with the world leads me to a vision of New Creation that impels my life.[6]

Such approaches keep alive the prophetic nature of the Word of God as a liberating and critical word, one which challenges existing social and religious practices and speaks on behalf of the outcasts.

Although this reading of the bible relies not simply on isolated texts, but on the bible's self-critical impulse, it does focus attention on passages from the prophets which call for conversion from injustice and action for a just world:

> **Amos 2:6–7.** Amos condemns the injustice of a society bent on wealth and prosperity, a society forgetful of God.

> They sell the just person for money
> and the poor for a pair of shoes,
> and trample the heads of the impoverished
> into the dust of the ground
> and shove the afflicted aside on the road.

Hosea 4:1–3. The prophet Hosea delivers a similar message.

Hear the word of God, people of Israel.
God has a lawsuit against the inhabitants of this land.
There is neither fidelity nor loving compassion,
and no knowledge of God in the land.
There is instead swearing oaths, lying, killing, stealing
and adultery;
there is violence and murder upon murder.
Therefore the land fails and all its inhabitants perish;
even wild beasts, birds of the air, and the fish in the sea
die.

Other sections of scripture enunciate this inclusive vision of life. We examined two of them in previous chapters:

Acts 17:26 and 28. This passage depicts the whole human race, including persons of all colors, religions, political and economic systems, as living, moving, and finding their existence within the cosmic womb of the one God.

Galatians 3:28. This is a baptismal fragment which points to the Christian community as one that embraces all races, religions and sexes in a discipleship of equals.

Scripture is experienced as God's word when it is heard in communities of faith; within these communities the Spirit empowers the word to convert hearts and heal societies. But the biblical word is itself in need of liberation from a patriarchal worldview. Our prayer is part of that process of liberation. The biblical words come alive most fully when they are heard and lived in communities struggling for freedom; this struggle frees the biblical words themselves from their own historical limitations.[7]

REMEMBERING AND MOURNING WOMEN'S PAIN

Remembering is an important part of the spiritual journey. Remembrance as scriptural prayer encompasses not only stories of good persons and the virtues that define their character, but also stories of shared suffering and of suffering inflicted on others. These stories cause us to mourn, cry out in protest, and seek reconciliation.

We cannot pray with scripture while pretending that it is not a sexist book. Our prayer must then come to terms with the tradition of oppression and the suffering of women found in the bible. For example, Phyllis Trible shows us how to remember and mourn with the biblical women found in what she calls *Texts of Terror:*[8]

> **Genesis 16:1–16.** The story of Hagar, the Egyptian slave who is Sarah's maid, a woman who is used to bear a child and then is abused and rejected.
>
> **2 Samuel 13:1–22.** The story of Tamar, the princess who is raped by her brother Amnon, and then is disgraced and isolated.
>
> **Judges 11:29–40.** The tale of the daughter of Jephthah, a virgin who is slain and sacrificed because of a vow her father chooses to make.

Memory of past oppression can serve as a motivating force in continuing the struggle against patriarchy, fueling efforts to eliminate such pain in the present and future.

A form of prayer especially apt for this process, one which is experiencing a revival today, is the prayer of lament. Lament gives voice to the experiences of pain, loss, and sorrow. It raises questions of justice in terms of social goods, social access and social power, and it keeps the justice question visible and legitimate. For these reasons, lament is a prayer especially appropriate for oppressed persons. It stands in contrast to a faith based on success and middle-class comforts, acquainted as lament is with failure, despair, and exhausting struggle.[9] When lament is absent from Christian life and liturgy, acceptable prayer can be confused with docility, submissiveness, and passive silence in the face of pain.

The biblical laments are dialogues of an individual or community with God in which they freely express their anger and grief. Some of these prayers may have been composed in a setting like that of a house church or a base community in which members enact a ritual as an act of hope.[10] Many of the laments are familiar to us, but hearing them again reminds us of their importance in personal and community prayer:

Psalm 44:23–26. A Community Lament.

> Wake up, God! Why are you asleep?
> Awake! Do not abandon us for good.
> Why do you hide your face,
> and forget that we are wretched and exploited?
>
> For we are bowed in the dust,
> our bodies crushed to the ground.
> Rise! Come to our help!
> Redeem us for the sake of your love.

Psalm 42:2,9. An Individual Lament.

> My soul thirsts for God
>   the God of life;
> When shall I go to see
>   the face of God?
>
> . . . .
>
> It is you, God, who are my shelter:
>   Why do you abandon me?
> Why must I walk
>   so mournfully, oppressed by the enemy?

As Walter Brueggemann notes, the laments are expressions of a relationship with God that is probing, pain-filled and in process.[11] They reflect a God of compassion who creatively responds to the processes of human history. In laments we articulate our pain fully and insist on God's reception of the speech and the pain. Laments are bold prayers that embrace risk. At the same time, they look forward to change and transformation:

> And now, what do I hope for?
>   My hope is in you.
>
> . . . .

> Hear my prayer, God
> to my cry give ear,
> at my tears do not be silent
>   for I am a sojourner with you. (Ps 39:7,12)

The basis of the lament is active hope and trust.

Several biblical laments are attributed to women. In 1 Samuel 1:10, Hannah prays when she is discriminated against by Elkanah because of her barrenness: "In the bitterness of her soul she prayed to God with many tears." Martha voices such a prayer to Jesus: "If you had been here, my brother would never have died!" (Jn 11:21).

In addition to using laments from the bible, women like to compose their own laments. Phyllis Trible provides a model at the conclusion of her discussion of Jephthah's sacrifice of his daughter. Here is its final section:

> Daughter of Jephthah, beloved and lovely!
>   In life and in death a virgin child,
> Greeting her father with music and dances,
>   facing his blame with clarity and strength.
>
> Ye daughters of Israel, weep for your sister,
>   who suffered the betrayal of her foolish father,
>   who turned to you for solace and love.
>
> How are the powerless fallen
>   in the midst of the victory!
>
> The daughter of Jephthah lies slain
>   upon thy high places.
> I weep for you, my little sister.
> Very poignant is your story to me;
>   your courage to me is wonderful,
>   surpassing the courage of men.
>
> How are the powerless fallen,
>   a terrible sacrifice to a faithless vow![12]

In developing your own laments you may find it useful to follow a simple structure that includes a lament's key elements:

(a) an address; (b) the lament and a petition; (c) an expression of assurance of being heard by God.

LISTENING TO THE SILENCES

Throughout scripture there are women who appear only in the shadows or who are just barely heard. In patriarchal writing, men are center stage; women are either invisible or appear peripherally. Behind the written text is a wealth of women's experience that has been largely overlooked. Reading the history of Israel, for example, we wonder what it would have been like if written from the perspective of the many wives and mothers who are named but never speak. One way in which women can dialogue with scripture passages in prayer is to bring their own experience as women to bear on the text, engaging in imaginative reconstruction of the lives of women mentioned there. This interaction with the text often results in new insights into our own faith experience as well as enlivening scripture for us. In a way such prayer has always been a part of prayer with scripture as we attempted to fill in the details of a biblical scene from historical background or human experience.

Judith Plaskow, speaking from the perspective of a Jewish woman, writes about the wife/sister stories in the book of Genesis. Three times, twice with reference to Abraham and once with reference to Isaac, the bible narrates that one of the patriarchs, during a famine in the land of Canaan, journeyed to a strange land with his wife in search of food. Each time the patriarch, afraid that the people of the land will kill him in order to marry his beautiful wife, asks her to say that she is his sister, in order that he might be treated well on her account. Referring to the invisibility of these women, Plaskow says: "We are using our power to reclaim our heritage in an ongoing *midrash* that places Sarah at the center. . . . We think we know something of what Sarah felt, and much more will we uncover and come to know."[13] As we tell and retell our own stories, we understand better how the women in these narratives would retell the biblical story if they could.

105

Some passages which women have used fruitfully for such
an approach are the following:

1. The reference to Miriam in Exodus 15:20–21. Read in
relationship with Numbers 20:1, Numbers 26:59, Deuteron-
omy 24:9, 1 Chronicles 5:29, and Michah 6:4.[14]

2. The story of Sarah in Genesis 18. Read in connection
with other comments on Sarah in Genesis 16:1–16 and Genesis 20–21, and Hebrews 11:11–12.[15]

3. The story of Bathsheba in 2 Samuel 11:1ff.

4. The reference to Anna in Luke 2:36–38.

5. The reference to Pilate's wife in Matthew 27:19.

Praying with such passages means using the imagination
to lift the curtain of silence surrounding these women. Some
questions can help such reflection:

1. How does this woman enrich the story of salvation?
2. What do you imagine this woman is thinking and feeling?
3. Respond for her to the situation.
4. Ask the woman some questions.
5. Tell her what you are feeling and thinking as you hear this
   story.
6. Where is the silence surrounding this woman repeated today? What responses arise in you in light of this silence?

Prayer that fills in the silences of the bible is based on the realization that the biblical text tells only part of the story. Wom-
en's contributions have been mostly excluded from the
written record.

In giving biblical women voice, it is also helpful to draw
out the implications of women's discipleship in the New
Testament. For example, women number themselves among
the crowd listening to Jesus' Sermon on the Mount. Likewise, we know that women were among those who gathered
when the Spirit descended in tongues of flame, as recounted
in Acts 2:1–4. Behind such a reading is the conviction that
women have always been disciples of Jesus; there were thus
many women among those who heard his preaching and
teaching. It helps to consider how women in the crowd
would have heard and responded to these words of Jesus.

106

Women follow Jesus from Galilee to Jerusalem, accompany him on the way to the cross, and witness his death. They are leaders and members of the early Christian communities. When the Christian community is addressed, women are at its center, not merely at its edges.

The development of inclusive biblical translations is critical for all efforts to bring women into greater prominence in the biblical record. Praying with only those passages which explicitly mention women leaves us feeling marginal. Such texts are limited, and patriarchy is pervasive. Since androcentric or male-centered language has functioned as inclusive language in the bible, women have rightly assumed that we were included even in biblical passages where no women are specifically mentioned. But the translation itself ought to make clear that women were present as well as men.[16]

We have explored several redemptive ways for women to read and pray the bible. Nevertheless there are some women who find that because of its sexism, they can no longer pray with scripture, and that for varying periods of time it is not helpful in their spiritual lives. They need to seek the word of God and the presence of God in other places. Many, like these two women, turn to other resources.

My main resources are the arts, literature, people's stories.

The bible is an important religious resource for me, though I find myself alternating between phases of reading and not reading it. In recent years I've gained a deeper understanding of biblical truths and their universality. Still and yet, biblical images dry up for me and I turn to novels, plays, and movies for images.

When the bible no longer speaks to women, they listen to the word of God in their own lives, in nature, in others' life stories, and in art or literature. Spiritual friends can help them learn how to listen for that presence, and trust the transformations it brings about.

107

One form of literature some women turn to is utopian fiction, novels such as Charlotte Perkins Gilman's *Herland,* Usula Le Guin's *The Left Hand of Darkness,* Doris Lessings's *The Marriages Between Zones Three, Four, and Five,* and Marge Piercy's *Woman on the Edge of Time.*[17] Utopian literature envisions alternative futures, futures that can influence present action for change. In addition, the world views implied in these works often inspire hope. In varying degrees they enflesh woman's faith in God's future.

FOR PRAYER AND REFLECTION

1. Guided Imagination: The Woman at the Well

Read: John 4:1–42

Quiet and relax your mind and body for a time.

Then imagine yourself in the Samaritan town called Sychar in central Palestine. It is noon on a warm day and you have come to draw water at the well. This well is dear to you because your foremothers drew water from it . . . You pause as you approach the well and look out at the broad fertile plain around the town. Feel the warmth of the noonday sun on your face. Take in the sweep of the plain.

You set your water jar down at the well, and notice a stranger seated there . . . Suddenly he says to you, "Give me a drink."

What are you thinking as he speaks these words? . . . What do you feel? . . . Do you give him a drink?

He speaks again and tells you that if you knew who he was, you would be asking him for water. His water becomes a life-giving inner spring.

How do these promises of living water and an inner spring of life affect you? . . . What hopes and longings do they evoke? . . . Are you thirsty? For what? . . . Do they give rise to any doubts and fears? . . . If so, what are they? Spend some moments with the thoughts and feelings these words produce in you.

You decide to ask for this water. What do you say to him? . . .

In reply he reveals to you an important truth about yourself that leaves you feeling known, yet loved. What does he tell you? . . .

His revelation to you calls up your hopes for the arrival of God's promises, and you tell him, "I know that the Messiah is coming." He replies, "I am he." How do these words strike you? . . . What arc you feeling as you hear them? . . .

As you are taking in his words, you hear voices and turn to see several men approaching. They seem surprised to find their friend talking to you, but they say nothing. Notice their faces as they look at you and at him.

You are not really interested in them. You set down your water jar and rush back to the town to tell people about this stranger. What do you say about him? . . . How do others respond? . . . What are you feeling as you share your good news with these people? . . . What do you discover about yourself as you take on this new role in your community? . . .

Spend a few moments in quiet prayer, and when you are ready, open your eyes.

2. Dancing Scripture

Needs: Room to move. Bible for each participant.

Begin with a movement warm-up. Choose some music that suits your mood and go through your body from foot to head exploring how each part moves and is connected to the surrounding parts of your body. In a group you can take turns leading movements with different body parts. Don't forget your spine!

After warming up, quiet yourself and breathe deeply. Begin to reflect on what life situation is foremost for you and name specifically what feelings this brings up in you. In a group, share your reflections with a partner, and with one another's help, identify a scripture passage that speaks to you with relation to your life.

Spend some time now reading and reflecting on your passage. Notice whom you identify with in the passage. Where in your body do you respond and with what feelings? Choose some music to support you. Spend ten to twenty minutes moving the feelings you have in response to the scripture. Exaggerate each expression so that your whole body is involved, whether that be twisting in pain and despair, reaching out in need, striding in conviction and power, bowing in humility, leaping in praise. If there are particular characters in your passage, actually become one or several of the characters and move their experiences. Do not focus on miming every action, but instead capture the quality of the character's feeling in movement. Remember, there is no right or wrong in this exercise!

If you are alone, write your discoveries in your journal. In a group setting, you may want to share portions of your readings and dances with one another. Keep in mind, this is not a performance! Witness each other in the atmosphere of shared prayer.
(This exercise was created by Betsey Beckman; see p. 48–49.)

3. Praying the Magnificat

One way to enter into the gospel vision of liberation is through the song of Mary in Luke 1:46–56. In it she affirms that God is faithful to the oppressed. She celebrates the power of God that transforms all our human divisions and categories. Meditate on Mary's song, or write your own song of liberation using the Magnificat as a model.

Like the psalms, the Magnificat is poetic speech. It unfolds in a circular way, and so requires repetition and a slow rhythm. Let its repetitive pattern deepen your mood and thought, allowing you to respond with your body and feelings as well as your mind.

110

[1]Three helpful collections of their work are *Feminist Perspectives on Biblical Scholarship*, ed. Adela Yarbro Collins (Chico: CA: Scholars Press, 1985); *The Bible and Feminist Hermeneutics. Semeia* 28, ed. Mary Ann Tolbert (Chico: CA: Scholars Press, 1983); *Feminist Interpretation of the Bible*, ed. Letty M. Russell (Philadelphia: Westminster Press, 1985). See also Elisabeth Schüssler Fiorenza, *Bread Not Stone. The Challenge of Feminist Biblical Interpretation* (Boston: Beacon Press, 1984).

[2]For a detailed discussion of this text see J. Cheryl Exum, " 'You Shall Let Every Daughter Live': A Study of Exodus 1:8–2:10," *The Bible and Feminist Hermeneutics*, pp. 63–82.

[3]"Tradition and Convention in the Book of Judith," *The Bible and Feminist Hermeneutics*, pp. 49–61.

[4]Elisabeth Schüssler Fiorenza, *In Memory of Her*, p. 320.

[5]See Rosemary Ruether, *Sexism and God-Talk*, p. 19.

[6]*Household of Freedom*, p. 138.

[7]See *Feminist Interpretation of the Bible*, ed. Letty M. Russell, pp. 17–18.

[8](Philadelphia: Fortress, 1984).

[9]See Beldon C. Lane, "Hutzpa K'Lapei Shamaya: A Christian Response to the Jewish Tradition of Arguing with God," *Journal of Ecumenical Studies* 23 (Fall 1986), 584.

[10]Walter Brueggemann, "The Costly Loss of Lament," *Journal for the Study of the Old Testament*, 36 (1986), 59. See also Jane Klimisch, O.S.B., "The Prayer of Lament: A Voice for Our Time," *The American Biblical Review* 37 (December 1986), 323–335.

[11]See "The Costly Loss of Lament."

[12]*Texts of Terror*, p. 109.

[13]"The Wife/Sister Stories: Dilemmas of the Jewish Feminist," in *Speaking of Faith*, p. 129.

[14]A helpful analysis of these texts can be found in Rita J. Burns, *Has the Lord Indeed Spoken Only Through Moses? A Study of the Biblical Portrait of Miriam* (Atlanta, GA: Scholars Press, 1987).

[15]See also Mary Callaway, *Sing, O Barren One: A Study In Comparative Midrash* (Atlanta, GA: Scholars Press, 1986).

[16]There are now a number of resources available which use or promote the use of inclusive language. See, for example, *The Liberating Word: A Guide to Non-Sexist Interpretation of the Bible,* ed. Letty M. Russell (Philadelphia: Westminster Press, 1976); *An Inclusive Language Lectionary: Readings for Year A (1983), Year B (1984), Year C (1985)* (Philadelphia: Westminster Press); Miriam Therese Winter, *Woman Prayer. Woman Song. Resources for Ritual* (Oak Park, IL: Meyer Stone Press, 1987).

[17]This literature is analyzed in *Women and Utopia. Critical Interpretations,* ed. Marleen Barr and Nicholas D. Smith (New York: University Press of America, 1983).

6

Discernment

Discernment is not simply one moment in the spiritual direction process. All of spiritual direction is discernment, since the goal of both is to help us become as closely attuned as possible to God's purposes for us, thereby discovering our own happiness as well. Spiritual direction, as the words indicate, concerns the direction or orientation we are choosing for our lives. Periods of major decision-making are really an intensification of our daily efforts to find the path to growth and holiness. Where are our decisions, both minor and major, leading us? Are we choosing life, moving toward greater personal wholeness and a more just and loving world? Or are we, consciously or unconsciously, strengthening the power of death and evil in our own lives and in society? What does God want us to be and do, and how is this related to what we want? Discernment is the process of attending to these and similar questions.

Discernment has never been easy; it is always marked by mystery and uncertainty. It is especially difficult for women today. Turning to tradition for confirmation of our decisions is problematic since that tradition has so often betrayed us. But if we cannot turn to tradition, where can we turn? What norms are there for distinguishing true and false spiritual growth?

The very circumstances that make discernment so difficult for us as women also make it more urgent. When established guideposts can no longer be trusted, and traditional
patterns are called into question, we need even more encouragement in our efforts to find the path to life. A young woman
reflects on her experience of this.

> When I try out new ways of being and acting, I find
> that nobody out there gives me the kind of positive
> response I've had before. I'm not used to having any-
> one dislike me. This is really hard. Sometimes I won-
> der, "Where is God in all of this?" Or else I think I'm
> just crazy to be going against the grain. I'm tempted
> to go back to the old ways of dealing with life; they
> seem so safe and comfortable.

Discernment is more important than ever in a world where
women and men are increasingly aware of the reality of oppression. It needs to be rethought in this new context.

In approaching discernment with women, I have found it
helpful to use several guidelines which take account of wom-
en's issues. I have formulated these as a checklist which a
woman can use to reflect on her own decisions, and which a
spiritual friend can have in mind as she listens to and supports
a woman's discernment process. The following are the eight
guidelines, with an explanation of each:

1. Listen to Your Deepest Self.

As Ernest Larkin points out in his fine study, *Silent Presence: Discernment as Process and Problem,* the movement of
God in our lives emerges as we come to know our deepest
selves. Larkin describes the process of finding God in our lives
in terms of this awareness of self.

> We are dealing with the real, our own experience, our
> own reason and judgment, our language, our world,
> and once we are deep enough into self-understanding,
> we simply know what to be "in attunement" to our-

114

selves means and when it does and does not exist. The language is not religious, but the reality is of God.[1]

When we come closest to the real, we are closest to God. It is also in the discovery of this inner truth that we are able to recognize our false selves.

This injunction to know the self and act from the deepest levels of the self is common in discussions of discernment. However, recent literature on woman's psychological development indicates that it can present special problems for women. In *A New Approach to Woman and Therapy*, Miriam Greenspan lists among the problems which most often bring women to therapy that (1) they doubt their own competence, and (2) they feel they have no sense of self at all.[2] Psychologist Jean Baker Miller would concur with Greenspan's findings, and reflects on the reasons for them.

> Almost from the moment of birth, there has been instilled in us the inner notion that acting out of one's self is a dangerous, frightening and evil thing. Although such actions are encouraged in men, and become very enchancing to men's sense of self, self-worth, and self-esteem—they have the reverse effect for many women: threatening one's sense of self and producing a sense of unworthiness, evil, danger—or, at the very least, a sense of conflict and unease. . . .
>
> This built-in threat has been a powerful force preventing most women from being able to connect freely with the first basic element of being alive—acting out of one's self and one's desires as one sees them at each moment. It then prevents us from being able to formulate, to know, and state our desires.[3]

The capacity to listen to one's deepest feelings and desires is not something that can be assumed in a woman's discernment process; it is, rather, a goal of spiritual direction.

Reaching this awareness of my own deepest wants involves a process of distinguishing them from extrinsic shoulds—what my parents want me to do, what will please others and meet their expectations—and from passing likes and dislikes, whims or feelings that do not really engage my personality.

Once women begin to answer the question "What do I most deeply want?" they then need to trust that this is also what God wants for them. Such trust rests on the conviction that being authentically myself and being the person God wants me to be are one and the same. Underlying this whole process is the premise that our selfhood is sacred. Until this level of self understanding and acceptance is reached, discernment will be affected by inadequate self-images. That is why so much of spiritual direction with women is concerned with developing a new way of imaging self.

Women do not typically need to hear the constant references to the dangers of self-love, selfishness, and self-centeredness which punctuate most discussions of discernment. In my experience, women do not usually choose the path of death rather than life because of self-love. Rather, as so much feminist literature makes clear, their choices go wrong because of an inability to love self well. Certainly women, like men, fail to love perfectly in concrete situations. But the roots of their failure lie less in overextension of the self than in a weak sense of any self at all. One manifestation of this is envy. As Madonna Kolbenschlag says well in *Kiss Sleeping Beauty Goodbye:*

> Envy flourishes in those who refuse to take up the burden of selfhood, in those who abdicate from their own uniqueness and power of creative action, above all in those who do not truly love themselves.[4]

Women's choices are frequently skewed by timidity and fear in face of autonomous action, self-hatred born of internalized oppression, and an anxiety that leads to evasion and helplessness.

Most traditional spiritual understandings of the annihilation of the ego, or the overcoming of self, are more appropriately applied to men than to women. Under patriarchy, male agency and authority are constantly validated. Men may therefore need to be aware of the dangers of control and domination, of the limits of the personal ego. But for women who do not have a strong sense of self in the first place, such approaches can reinforce forms of self-abnegation that they are already engaging in to their own detriment. After centuries of having their lives defined and controlled by others, women need help in achieving some self-direction.

Women's formation inclines them to a reflective identity, one that is mediated by others and will be of benefit to others. This means that they mirror the desires and feelings of those close to them, losing in the meantime a sense of their own. During a discussion of possible ministry options, a young woman commented:

> I suppose what I am really struggling with is to accept myself instead of depending on outsiders to determine my worth. That is such a hard place to get to.

Women do have a false self which they must relinquish in order to find the path to life. But it is not the ego, as this is usually understood, which stands in their way. Perhaps what women need to die to is the false system imposed on them by patriarchy, whatever form that has taken in their lives; dying to this false self would prepare for the birth of their true selves. Men, on the other hand, may need to die to a self experienced as separate and distinct from others, and be reborn into relationality.[5]

2. Affirm Your Own As Well As Others' Needs.

Another challenge women face is to affirm *both* the fullest development of themselves and the nurturing of relationships, in other words, to learn what it means in practice to be a self-in-relation. This can be an area of special difficulty in discernment. Two women describe the dilemma.

> I'm still struggling. To love one's neighbor as oneself presupposes love of self. Real love is built on integrity and justice, not door-mat servility. But there is a pre-

carious balance—I struggle to believe it is OK to pay attention to myself, but I also am wary of the siren song of overdoing self-awareness, self-service, consciousness raising, and neglecting legitimate forms of self-denial in my family.

That conflict was a great struggle particularly last year when I began the spiritual direction that began the healing. Taking care of myself before others is against everything I was brought up on. I was helped to see that it was a matter of life and death for me. So I undertook it as a project in healing, in reclaiming my body/being. The conflict still rears its head but I have come to believe I can't be for others unless I take care of myself and set some limits. I think the conflict will always be there. I am trying to grow in my ability to be in touch with who I am and to be able to discern in that light the appropriate thing to do for my own being.

Like many other women, the women quoted above began to see that self and other are interdependent, that the two loves are interwoven.

Insights from the research of Carol Gilligan and others correlate well with the statements of these women. Gilligan's *In a Different Voice* shows how women's identity is defined in a context of relationships and judged by a standard of responsibility and care.[6] Whereas the male "I" is defined in separation, women develop in a context of attachment and affiliation with others. Women's sense of self is so organized around making and maintaining relationships, that disruption of such relationships is perceived not just as the loss of the relationship, but closer to a total loss of the self. Conflicting commitments to self and other converge in the discovery of the connection between social responsibility and self-care.

The authors of *Women and Self-Esteem* write along these same lines when they describe the goal of feminist therapy:

To help women find out who we are and to value who we are, and to do this without giving up the qualities

118

of kindness, nurturance, empathy and concern for human relationships that our special socialization usually equips us with.[7]

Since woman's conception of self is rooted in a sense of connection and relatedness to others, her discernment will reflect this way of knowing. It will be a continual effort to relate her sense of self to the making and maintaining of relationships. Knowing is itself a process of human relationship; it is "connected knowing."[8] This is as true of discernment as of other modes of knowing.

The process of discernment has not been helped by world views which assume a dichotomy between self and others. Within such a world view women have been led to believe that they must choose between relationships, the "we" in their lives, and the self or "I". In an interdependent world view it is possible to have both. As one woman said, "I know I can care and not be submerged." Situated within an interdependent world view, the question for discernment in concrete instances of loving is no longer: Should I love myself or others? Rather, the assumption is that I cannot love one well without loving the other. This transforms the questions for discernment to ones such as: How will I choose to care for both self and others in this situation? Sacrificing the self for the relationship is not necessarily the choice of love. Discernment may lead to the conviction that the pattern of the relationship itself must be transformed or restructured.

An example may help make this clear. A woman in her seventies was trying to discover the course of action she should take regarding her husband's care. She was a strong and loving woman who had raised seven children and was now attempting to care for her husband in the advanced stages of Alzheimer's disease. She had prayed and prayed, she said, that God would enable her to care for him. In spite of the exhausting demands of such care, she felt guilty when she noticed within herself feelings of resentment and anger toward her husband. These must be signs of her own selfishness, she thought. Her children begged her to let them help in the care, and urged her to get out of the house and maintain contact with her friends and activities. However, if her husband protested when she attempted to leave, she would change her plans and stay home. Her sense of fidelity to him was very strong.

What did God want of her in this situation? she asked. Was she sinning by feeling the way she did about her husband? Would it violate her promise of faithfulness to him if she turned over some of his care to others? Later, as she moved toward a decision to accept help with his care, she said that two convictions were especially helpful to her: the realization that the better she cared for herself, the better she would be able to care for her husband; and the insight that she would be extending, not relinquishing, the circle of love and care by letting others help with her husband. She also had to hear her anger and resentment not as sinful feelings, but as a sign that she was not taking sufficient care of *herself*.

3. *Do Not Confuse Passivity with Conformity to God's Will.*

In the New Testament the life of Jesus is summed up as doing God's will. This has also been the ideal of the spiritual life throughout the centuries. Not only do we want to be open to the presence of God in our lives, we want to align our actions with God's purposes in the world. This means openness to knowing God's will for us.

In this process, certain false conceptions of God's will can reinforce negative cultural conditioning in women. One such conception equates God's will with external authority; finding God's will then means trying to measure up to that outer authority rather than developing a sense of inner authority. Women can mistakenly think they are living out God's will when they are merely living out of a cultural pattern of conformity or helplessness.

Some insights from recent psychological research provide a context for understanding the significance of this aspect of discernment for women. Research on women and depression shows that (1) women are two to three times more likely to experience depression than men, and (2) depression is a response to being out of control in one's life.[9] Depression is often the consequence of experiencing little connection between actions we initiate and what happens to us. It results from feeling helpless and powerless, from submitting to unfair circumstances and then denying the anger we feel as a result or blaming ourselves for our feelings of unhappiness and futility. Why should depression be a concern of spiritual direction? The symptoms of depression are death in life: a sense of loss and helplessness, absence of energy and joy. The Christian call is exactly the opposite: resurrection and new life.

There is a second way in which confusion about God's will leads to passivity in women. That is the supposition that God's will is a detailed plan for every aspect of our lives, so that discernment is not a matter of adult reflection and decision, but a feat of finding the hidden preplan and then simply conforming to it. God's purpose is not a detailed plan for our lives, but rather a general call to the fullness of what we and the world might become.[10] In a situation where many choices are possible, it is not necessary to search for one single way as God's will. Discernment to know God's purpose is openness to a direction, a fullness of possibility. Any of several options might express that direction. Finding God's will is a matter of making the best creative choice I can make within a given set of circumstances. God leaves the specifics up to me.

God's purpose, then, is not set over against my autonomy and desires; rather it dwells within and is revealed in my deepest feelings and context. Taking charge of my life is one of the ways in which I live out this will as it is gradually revealed to me. This revelation comes in terms of the options open to me in my actual life situation. Attunement to God's purpose is therefore an ongoing process, not a finished action. There is no guarantee of freedom from illusion and uncertainty, since we can never fully know God's will or purpose.

4. Trust the Insights That Come From Your Body, Intuition, and Feelings.

A focus on listening to the guidance of the Spirit within can help women move to inner-directedness and freedom from the kind of outer-directedness that relies solely on others for the norms of decision-making. But it calls for attentiveness to *all* dimensions of the self, the emotional as well as the rational, the conscious as well as the unconscious. The resources stressed in this approach to discernment are ones which women's socialization has strengthened in them: intuition, bodily awareness, imagination, empathy.

Since our culture has often devalued these gifts, women themselves may fail to utilize them fully in discernment. The commonly accepted stereotype of women's thinking as emotional and intuitive contributes to the eclipse of these forms of knowing in Western technological societies which value rationalism and objectivity. When a woman comes to me for help with discernment having prepared a list of pros and cons for taking certain actions, I usually focus my listening primarily on the emotions and body messages she conveys as she presents each list. I reflect these back to her. At these levels she often already knows what her decision is, even though she has difficulty trusting it.

Although intuition is frequently considered primitive and therefore unreliable, intuitive knowing—experienced and felt rather than thought out—can be an important bearer of truth. God's truth is always embodied. As Denise Levertov says in the final lines of her poem, "Variation and Reflection on a Theme by Rilke":

> Within the pulse of flesh,
> in the dust of being, where we trudge,
>   turning our hungry gaze this way and that,
> the wings of the morning
> brush through our blood
> as cloud-shadows brush the land.
> What we desire travels with us.
> We must breathe time as fishes breathe water.
> God's flight circles us.[11]

God's word is always shrouded in mystery; we hear it, as T.S. Eliot suggests, only in "hints and guesses."

Several of the ordained ministers interviewed by Lynn Rhodes for her book *Co-Creating: A Feminist Vision of Ministry* attest to the power of intuition in their lives. One of them finds it especially helpful for discerning what is happening during meetings with church officials and colleagues.

> I have learned over time to pay close attention to my instinct in those meetings. I used to dismiss my feelings of unease because I did not have immediate verbal responses, but I've discovered that I need to pay attention to my instinct—something is usually going on that is not being acknowledged.[12]

Another woman minister finds that her intuition provides the initial clues to confusing situations. Reflecting on these feelings provides important insights for her work. Once women begin to trust their intuitive processes, they find they have tapped one of their most valuable resources for discernment.

5. Be Aware of the Social and Cultural Forces Influencing a Situation.

Many discussions of discernment place all the emphasis on awareness of inner states and the process of sifting through our affective experiences. This is good, but the focus of interest needs to be broadened. It must include outer circumstances, social arrangements, and structures. It must situate our personal histories within cultural and religious history.[13]

In discernment we seek a graced awareness of how we are to respond to God's invitation in a concrete situation. That response may be a prophetic one, in tension with prevailing structures. Approaches to discernment need to be based on the realization that healing society's inequities is the only lasting way to bring about spiritual wholeness for all persons.

This calls for social analysis. It is particularly important for the process of discernment by women. In this model discernment still begins with experience, listening to the Spirit in self and world and becoming aware of what one hears. Social analysis adds a next step to this. If I feel the call of the Spirit to a fuller ministry in the church, why is it that I cannot live out that call? Is the situation as it stands God's will? Why must I struggle so hard as a single mother to make enough money to support my children? What are the forces influencing my life and determining the kind of opportunities I will have, what I can earn, what choices I have? The action which follows from this kind of discernment reflects a more complete sense of all the factors influencing a decision.

As an illustration of this point, consider the discernment of a woman in her late thirties, the mother of three children just approaching their teen years. She had been praying about a decision to continue a program to prepare her to do ministry in the church. When she thought about following the program, she was aware of strong feelings of joy and enthusiasm. She knew from experience how depressed she was when she stayed home and focused only on such concerns as planning meals and taking the kids to swimming lessons. Yet these were also very important realities for her. Her enthusiasm was clouded by distress, because she knew that studying left her less available to her husband and children than they wanted her to be. This created stress and conflict in the family. As she became aware of these different movements within herself, it helped this woman to do some analysis of the structures affecting her choice. Why was it that pay for church ministry was so low that she could not hope to see it as an economic help to her family? Could she bring about some changes in that situation and did she still want to choose it if she could not? Were the expectations in her marriage and family necessary ones or were there other ways of living out marriage and family life, ones more compatible with the call she was feeling to education and ministry? Such analysis provided the basis for deciding what she would do and how she would challenge the existing structures to make it possible for her to do what she saw as good.

6. Interpret Your Affective Experiences in Light of Women's Social Conditioning.

Social analysis not only adds a further step to our discernment process; it is integral as well to the use of affective criteria in discernment. If emotions are to offer clues to the influence of the good or evil spirit in our life, we must be aware of the way in which the experience of oppression has conditioned these emotional responses. As noted in our earlier reflections on women's spirituality, traditional accounts of holiness associate only certain affections, such as gentleness and devotion, with women. Many women then feel guilty if their choices lead to conflict.

Discernment with women requires recognition of the constructive aspects of conflict. The goal of discernment is growth in the Spirit, not the maintenance of the present social or religious system. Movement to the new brings conflict all along the way. Such conflict may decrease integration and temporarily heighten individual and social disorder, but it may benefit both in the long run. Conflict can be a regenerative force, leading to new life. Short-term discomfort may be necessary for moving out of destructive situations. In all of these areas spiritual friends can be a valuable resource, since it is difficult to find our way alone, and to know which aspects of conflict are appropriate and which are nonproductive.

Some of the most helpful guidance for distinguishing affective states is found in the Ignatian rules for discernment.[14] One of Ignatius' insights on how affective states are indicators of our life-direction can be especially helpful here. Ignatius describes consolation as the interior movement that indicates a direction toward God; desolation indicates a movement away from God. However, consolation and desolation are not necessarily to be identified with pleasure and pain. Consolation can be a peaceful feeling that is not entirely comfortable and pleasant. It is often a sense of rightness that runs deeper than surface emotions. Certain kinds of false guilt and discomfort which women experience when they go against cultural norms for them must not then be mistaken for desolation, that is, a sign that one is moving away from God. It may be necessary for a woman to live with false guilt for a time to find the way to life. The painful dimension can be accompanied by a pervasive feeling that this is right for me; this is what I must do even though it makes me feel uncomfortable.

For example, a very talented woman realized during the course of a retreat that she had lost her zest for life and ministry. In reviewing her professional life she saw that she had been repeatedly passed over and disregarded. She was an excellent teacher, loved by her students. But whenever recognition or special considerations were handed out, they went to less qualified male members of her department. When this happened, she felt some anger and resentment, but passed it over in the interests of being considered a good department member. She felt increasingly depressed, lacking in energy, and hopeless. Her love of teaching and her ability to help students were being eroded. Praying over this situation during retreat, she came to the awareness that she was allowing other persons to chart the course of her life for her. Their recognition and permission became the norms for what she could do. As a result of her prayer she began to assume responsibility for her own future. She continued to try to work well with her department, but not only on others' terms. She refused those assignments that merely put her in a subservient role, and undertook projects that allowed her to use her best gifts in a free and creative way. She hated the conflict and tension this caused and the disapproval she experienced from others. At the same time, on a deeper level she felt a sense of peace and wholeness about these decisions. In finding her own authority and freedom, she was convinced that she had also found what God values.

7. Try to Generate Alternatives When You Feel Trapped.

Discernment frequently leads to awareness of the need for transformative action; it therefore presupposes alternatives. An important part of discernment for oppressed persons is the generating of these alternatives, since they very often feel confined by available choices. This constriction can result from job discrimination, limited educational opportunities, lack of information, or lack of alternative role models. Imaging a different way of living is the first step toward change.

When women's choices are circumscribed by existing patterns, it is helpful to brainstorm other possibilities. This is best done in collaboration with others, since imagining with a community leads to possibilities we might not have seen alone. If even one thing can change, the context for decisions becomes a new one.

This aspect of discernment is also based on the realization that not all approaches work well in every situation. In the struggle for justice, for example, individuals need to choose the strategies that fit with their own personal gifts as well as the contexts in which they live. This means the rejection of some avenues and the opening up of others.

The courage to search for alternatives comes from realizing that the Spirit of God sets us free. Since the process of discernment is an attempt to know and follow the guidance of the Spirit in our lives, how we view the Spirit has a major influence on how we go about discernment. Fresh insights on the theology of the Spirit are coming to us today. Elisabeth Fiorenza describes the Spirit as a liberating force in our lives. She reminds us in *In Memory of Her* that the Lord is Spirit (Sophia) and brings freedom; whereever the Spirit of the Lord is, there is freedom (2 Cor 3:17).

The power of evil spirits can be seen in structures which impoverish human beings, holding them in bondage to the past. The Spirit of Christ frees us from the past.

> Therefore if anyone is in Christ, they are a new creation. The old has passed away, behold the new has come. (2 Cor 5:17)

When the cumulative weight of the past denies the richness of well-being to persons, it is demonic. As Fiorenza says,

> The true spiritual person is according to Paul the one who *walks* in the Spirit, she who brings about this new world and family of God over against the resistance and pull of all oppressive powers of the world's enslaving patriarchal structures.[15]

The newness that breaks into time with Jesus Christ seeks to transform the face of the earth.

8. Take Account of the Price of Change.

Insight is not usually sufficient to bring about change. I have been present with women as they saw clearly how personal and cultural patterns of thinking and acting contributed to their unhappiness. They could also see a way out, and knew what they had to do. But they felt unable to do it. They were aware that they stood at the line between life and death, and could move forward or slip back again into the patterns they were trying to leave behind. They could refuse to challenge oppression.

This is a time for relying deeply on God's grace, asking her to be with us as we step over into life. We may have to cross the border between life and death many times over the course of months or years before we finally choose to stay in the zone of life. It is not easy to change established social structures or the personal patterns of a lifetime, and this is what most women are dealing with when they begin to confront the sources of their unhappiness. Liberation is a conversion process, and it is God's work as well as our own.

We opened this chapter with a key question for discernment: What does God want us to be and do, and how is this related to what we want? Underlying the chapter's eight guidelines for approaching this question is a fundamental conviction: Whatever promotes the full humanity of women as well as men is redemptive and holy, that is, it is of God. What denies and distorts that full humanity does not bear the power and authority of divine revelation.[16] A word that calls every person—all genders, social groups, and races—to full dignity and happiness, this is indeed a word of life to guide our decision-making and commitments. Such a word frees us from falsehood and awakens us to love. And that, finally, is the goal of discernment.

FOR PRAYER AND REFLECTION

1. Woman as Image of God

This meditation substitutes positive statements about reality for some of the negative ideas and images which shape our attitudes and expectations toward life. As a way of affirming that we image God, and of resting in the divine core of our being, they prepare us for discernment. The statements can be done silently, spoken aloud, written down, sung or chanted.

Relax, breathe deeply and come to a quiet place within you. Light a candle and incense if you wish. You may also like to add some favorite music.

Choose one of these affirmations, or create your own, and slowly repeat it again and again. You might want to use several of the statements, pausing between them and coming back to any that are especially important to you.

I am a strong and creative woman.
I am made in the image of God.
I am a Co-Creator with God.
God dwells within me.
I live in oneness with all life.
I am a channel of God's healing power.

2. Discernment and the Reign of God: A Journal Exercise

The reign or realm of God is the norm by which we are to judge our present attitudes and actions. It is a vision of what God wants us and our world to be.

Take the reign of God as the subject of your prayer and reflection. Enter into these or other parables of Jesus and experience what the reign is like and what it demands of us.

Luke 14:16–24   The Great Feast: a festive banquet to which all are invited.

Matthew 20:1–16   The Laborers in the Vineyard: God's gracious goodness establishes equality and solidarity among us all.

Because a parable is a poetic metaphor, the purpose of our prayer is not to solve or explain it. Rather, we want to contemplate the parable from within, living in its details, identifying with its different characters, and letting it interpret and change us.

3. Group Support for Individual Discernment

Women in a circle or group can help one another with the social analysis which is part of discernment through the following steps. This is not an exercise in communal discernment, but rather a way in which a group can support the discernment process of individual women.

Open with a prayer to God as Sophia and Spirit. Ask for receptivity to the divine power within and in our midst. Then follow the three steps below.

a. Begin with the woman telling her story. As she tells her story, others in the group can share similar experiences and feelings, as well as ways they have dealt with them.

b. Together identify those aspects of the woman's experience that are unique to her as a woman, i.e., those dimensions that would not exist if she were a man or that are common to many women. This includes examining the role of the church as it relates to the woman's situation.

c. Suggest some creative choices. First the woman and then others in the group state the possible concrete paths she might take in light of her situation.

¹(Denville, NJ: Dimension Books, 1981), p. 47. See also Thomas Hart, *The Art of Christian Listening;* Karl Rahner, *The Dynamic Element in the Church* (New York: Herder & Herder, 1964); William C. Spohn, S.J., "The Reasoning Heart: An American Approach to Christian Discernment," *Theological Studies* 44 (March 1983), 30–53.

²P. 3.

³"The Necessity of Conflict," in *Women Changing Therapy,* p. 5.

⁴P. 51.

⁵This suggestion is made by Demaris Wehr in *Jung and Feminism,* pp. 100–103.

⁶(Cambridge, MA: Harvard University Press, 1982).

⁷Linda Tschirhart Sanford and Mary Ellen Donovan, *Women and Self-Esteem* (New York: Anchor Press/Doubleday, 1984), p. 259.

⁸See *Women's Ways of Knowing.*

⁹See Alexandra G. Kaplan, "The 'Self-In-Relation': Implications for Depression in Women," *Work in Progress* (Wellesley, MA: Stone Center For Developmental Services and Studies, 1984). Kaplan uses self in relation theory to move beyond our current understanding of depression in women.

¹⁰My understanding of God's will or purpose is based on process modes of thought, as developed by Alfred North Whitehead and others.

¹¹*Breathing the Water,* p. 83.

¹²(Philadelphia: Westminster Press, 1987), p. 33.

¹³See, for example, *Soul Friend,* pp. 132ff.; and *Women's Consciousness, Women's Conscience. A Reader in Feminist Ethics,* ed. Barbara Hilkert Andolsen, Christine E. Gudorf, and Mary D. Pellauer (San Francisco: Harper & Row, 1985).

¹⁴See Elisabeth Tetlow, "An Inclusive-Language Transla-

tion of the Ignatian Rules for Discernment," in *Women's Spirituality: Resources for Christian Development*, pp. 219–225.

[15]*In Memory of Her*, p. 346.

[16]For a development of this principle, see the essays by Margaret A. Farley and Rosemary Ruether in *Feminist Interpretation of the Bible*, ed. Letty Russell.

7

Women and Power

Many women become uncomfortable, even fearful, when the topic of power is introduced. Power connotes the use of ambition and force, subjects incompatible with Christian spirituality. Exercising power appears contrary to the gospel ideals of serving others and seeking the last place. It may even be destructive and harmful.

Yet the experience of powerlessness which results from woman's subordinate place in church and society is at the heart of many of our spiritual struggles. Issues of power arise daily in our personal relationships, our marriages, our ministry, and our efforts to work for a just society. On a personal level, integrity and happiness depend on our ability to exercise some control over events, to be agents in our lives. On a larger scale, power is a key issue in salvation and liberation, integral to hope and action for a better world. For these reasons the question of power is central, not peripheral, to spirituality.

This becomes clear as women reflect on their spiritual lives. In describing her faith questions, a young woman who has served for eight years as a professional minister in an urban parish, and hopes to pastor a parish some day, says:

I have several concerns regarding women in ministry right now and I have to watch carefully as I serve professionally not to get trapped by the hierarchical lay stuff, "I'm more priestly than the women in the pews" syndrome. My fear is that as we become professional leaders in the church, we will fall back into these hierarchical dichotomies, trichotomies. That does worry me. We need networks of support, training, in the feminine use of power.

Another woman expresses her concern in relation to authority, or legitimated power:

Being a Roman Catholic I find it particularly difficult to handle having relatively old, unmarried men isolated in the Vatican telling me—a married woman— what is or isn't acceptable (sinful) regarding treatment of my body, marriage, and sexual practices.

Women bring to spiritual direction a variety of other issues related to power, which can be summarized as follows:

If they attempt to speak up at work or in class they find their contributions, like their accomplishments, ignored or devalued.

Their husbands control the money or make all the decisions in their marriages and they feel they are being treated like children.

They are distressed by the competitiveness between women, as well as that between women and men.

They are angry that women are not treated as equals in the church and are denied opportunities to use their gifts or assume leadership roles.

They disapprove of the attempts of other women to use power, fearing that these women will arouse hostility or that the same changes will be expected of them.

They remain in jobs below their skills or level of education, but do not know how to take action on their own behalf.

Concerns centering around issues of power are no doubt among the most challenging ones women bring to spiritual direction today.

Although distressed and angered by the powerlessness they experience, many women feel helpless to do anything about it. When asked what they would do to change it, they reply: "I don't know how to change it." "I don't see how it *can* be changed." "I can't change it. It would truly be an act of God for the attitude of superiority to be transformed." Their comments underscore how complex these issues of power and powerlessness are, and how deeply they are embedded in present structures. They also point out once again the need for action at the political as well as the personal level.

Spiritual direction can support women's efforts to deal with this difficult issue. It does this by contributing to three essential tasks: (1) redefining power, (2) affirming ways in which women are already using power, and (3) developing strategies for an even fuller exercise of power. These tasks relate to areas that have always been a part of spiritual direction: clarification, encouragement, and discernment. Their goal is movement beyond the dichotomies of weak and strong which have split the reality of power into oppressive categories.

REDEFINING POWER

Many of our problems with power stem from faulty definitions. An insistence on polarities characterizes prevailing definitions of power; the poles of powerful and weak are equated with masculine and feminine and with governors and governed. Male equals power and strength, and female equals weakness and submission. Spiritual direction provides an op-

135

portunity to explore how we think about power and to alter that conception if we wish. By dealing directly with the topic we can contribute to new concepts and future uses of power. This clarification process for Christian women includes an understanding of servant power, the ideal based on Jesus as suffering servant which is offered to the Christian community as its paradigm for power.

Psychologist Jean Baker Miller considers dialogue to be an essential aspect of coming to terms with our difficulties regarding power.

> If we are really going to build the kinds of institutions and personal lives that allow women to grow and flourish, I believe that we must invest much more conscious, concerted, direct attention to women and power. At the same time I believe that most of us women still have a great deal of trouble with the whole area. The only hope, it seems to me, is to keep trying to examine it together.[1]

Our lives have been dominated by one conception of power. There is great validity, Miller believes, in our reluctance to use power as it is presently conceived and exercised. As women we have experienced satisfaction from helping others learn to develop their own capacities. Therefore we want to be powerful in a way that simultaneously enhances, rather than diminishes, the power of others.

The attempt to redefine power is producing helpful developments.[2] Several of these shifts are key elements in understanding women's relationship to power:

(1) Power is being viewed as a process of interaction between persons, not as a quality possessed by any single individual.

Previous depictions of power often presented it as an entity or thing, something possessed by individual persons. On this view, some people are powerful, some are not. When power is thus defined as an attribute of the powerful, inroads on that power are seen as serious encroachments to be resisted.

Any increase in power by one person necessarily entails a loss of power by the other.

Current focus is on power as an ever present and fluid component of relationships among persons. There is power operating whenever two or more people are interacting. To be in relationship, therefore, is to be involved in an exercise of power in some way. We cannot avoid it; what we can do is learn to make it a constructive rather than destructive process for everyone involved. Since power is not a quality of persons but a process of interaction among persons, it cannot be divided, assigning women power in some spheres such as the family while assigning men power in the public arena. It is not a matter of giving women power, as though it were an entity they did not already possess; it is, rather, a question of encouraging women to reclaim the power in relationships that is already theirs.

A similar emphasis on social process marks discussions of authority. Authority and power are frequently used interchangeably; although closely related, they are not identical. James and Evelyn Whitehead distinguish the two in a helpful way in *The Emerging Laity*.[3] They describe authority as that understanding of power which is explicit and legitimate among us. This power is explicit in that members of a group are generally aware that this is how things *do* operate; and it is legitimate insofar as members acknowledge this as the way things *should* operate. Our language tends to objectify authority just as it does power, making it a thing belonging to a particular person. Like power, however, authority is a social process, a relationship among persons. It is the community which prevents the excessive and destructive uses of power, whether this community be a partnership or a gathering of individuals.

[2] The paradigm of power as domination is being replaced by a paradigm of power as mutual influence.

We are in the midst of a major shift in our paradigms for power. The conception of power most familiar to us is derived from dominant/subordinate relationships; it has been termed

137

hierarchical or unilateral power. A new paradigm of power is emerging, one based on relationships of mutuality.

Examples of the power of dominance are not hard to find. It is present in a marriage relationship when the husband makes all the decisions, even those which directly affect his wife, with little or no input from her. In a work setting unilateral power decrees that those in charge issue orders while subordinates obey them. Much of the world's political exchange consists of power plays between superpowers. Those women who belong to churches with hierarchical power structures will recognize in these hierarchies many of the characteristics of unilateral power. Refusals of those who exercise hierarchical power to listen to other views stem from the fear that this will mean a loss of authority or power.

Unilateral or hierarchical power is a one-directional flow of influence. Being influenced is a sign of weakness. In other words, this paradigm of power is nonmutual and based on a noncommunal view of the self. The person influencing another is not open to being influenced in return. Identity and worth depend instead on being able to carry out our purposes in relation to the competing claims of others; we are judged by the amount of competing power we can resist or overcome. The distaste and fear of power which many women have relates to this kind of power.

There is, however, another way of conceptualizing power, power as relation and mutuality. It esteems both the ability to influence others and the capacity to be influenced by them. Relational power encompasses receiving as well as giving; speaking and listening are both creative aspects of a relationship. Power rooted in mutuality is the capacity to sustain a relationship in which both persons are really changed.

Relational power leads to collaboration rather than competition. There will always be inequalities in life, but within a notion of power where influence is mutual, inequalities do not become injustices. Such a view of power also fosters greater wholeness. Instead of rejecting what we consider to be weaknesses and projecting them onto others, we are able to hold these contrasts within our own unity. Basic to paradigms

138

of mutual power is the conviction that diversity need not be construed as threatening; it can be seen as enrichment.

(3) New approaches to power are giving rise to fresh images and metaphors.

Just as the power of domination is usually imaged as a pyramid or ladder, so the power of mutuality is compared to webs, nets, and gossamer threads. In a web, no one position dominates over another. Each person has some potential for influence on others and each is affected by the actions of others. The same is true of nets.

In the image of the net, even the least can affect all others by the slightest pull on the gossamer thread.[4]

Such images attempt to capture the bonds that knit human relationships together. In view of these bonds, it is not necessarily more blessed to give than to receive. The goal is for all persons, women and men alike, to learn both to give and to receive. Such power is also imaged as a circle in which the energy moves among all persons rather than from top to bottom; power is no longer exercised above or over others.

One illustration of the exercise of this kind of power comes from the women's peace camp at Greenham Common. In September 1981, women and children marched 120 miles from Cardiff to Greenham Common to set up a peace camp outside the U.S. air base there. On December 1982 more than 30,000 women came for an international celebration and protest at the base. The women were finally evicted and loads of boulders dumped where their camp had stood. In response to these power tactics of the authorities, the women developed tactics of their own. They spun webs of yarn on the perimeter fence to remind those inside of their presence. Later wool webs were used to entangle machinery, to string supine protesters together, and to befuddle police officers who had been trained to make armed charges but not to unravel knitting.[5]

139

(4) A new way of viewing our relationship with God grounds this new notion of power.

Our covenant with God is a partnership of mutuality, not a relationship of dominance and submission. Rather than being unaffected by our human lives and hopes, God really enters into relationships. A woman makes the point out of her own developing experience.

> I see my relation to God as one of increasing mutuality—God needs me and I need God. God desires relationship, and for that to happen, two identities are required.

In this view, God's perfection does not consist in being invulnerable and exercising external control. God shares in our sufferings, and also genuinely needs human collaboration to achieve the divine purpose.

The Hasidic tradition emphasizes the responsibility this mutual dependence places on humanity to bring liberation within the realm of history. According to the Hasidim, as a result of the entrance of sin into history in the Fall, divine sparks were scattered to the ends of creation. It is the task of humanity to gather these sparks back together into one unity. Any deed of reconciliation and love will aid in this task of recreation. The Hasidic image captures the call for human action implicit in this view of God's relationship to the world. We are co-creators with others and God, active agents in bringing about the future.

Changing paradigms of power also affect the way we image Jesus as servant. Rhetoric about servanthood has often been used against women, trapping them in subservient roles. Power based on mutual relationships provides a more helpful way of conceptualizing the servant power of Jesus. As suffering servant Jesus exercised power in the service of relationships, affirming the dignity and worth of each individual. He empowered others, unlocking their deepest desires and enabling them to use their best gifts.

Even Jesus the suffering servant did not passively submit

to the powers of his age. His death resulted from his efforts actively to change the course of human history. Jesus was suffering servant because he attempted to reconcile the forces of love and hatred. Some women find this expressed in a helpful way in an image from Ephesians 2:11–22, that of God having broken down in Jesus the dividing wall of hostility. Jesus calls both women and men to the genuine strength which is born of the power of relationship.

AFFIRMING WOMEN'S PERSONAL POWER

We move now from general considerations of power to their specific implications for women. Women have, in fact, already been exercising a distinct kind of power. However, because such power has not been affirmed by church and society, they may be unaware of it or discount it themselves. The characteristics most fully developed in women are frequently dysfunctional for success in the world as it is. However, as is clear from our reflections on redefining power, these qualities may be essential for human beings and for bringing about change in the world.[6] We need to begin to think of this power in terms of its usefulness for the world. It has the capacity to break down polarization and dichotomy and foster community. How have women been exercising power already? And what human models can we appeal to for inspiring an even broader use of our power?

Much of women's influence or power has been directed toward empowering others. Such power has been stereotyped as passivity. However, it need not be seen in this way. The receptivity intrinsic to empowering others is active openness. The contemporary American sculptor and poet, Liliane Lijn, describes it from the perspective of an artist.

The act of receiving, the passive act, is in essence active the moment it is accomplished with awareness. It is this specific awareness which is the particular characteristic and moreover the function of the artist. Call it attention, care, love. . . . I speak of a way of receiving which I consider whole. At once passive and active. Passive in that its receiving is an acceptance as opposed to a taking. Active in its attention and its ability to focus.[7]

Women find the exercise of power more satisfying if it simultaneously enhances the lives of others. Roles and careers traditionally assigned to women presuppose such attention to developing and nurturing others' gifts: motherhood, teaching, nursing. Enabling others is a central goal of women in ministry. Yet this is real power.

Many developmental theories emphasize the importance of disconnecting from relationships in order to form a separate sense of self. In contrast, current models of women's development stress that women's core self-structure or primary motivation is toward growth in relationships. These models affirm women's ways of becoming attuned to others' emotional states, their capacity for understanding and being understood by others. These are all ways of participating in the development of others. Such qualities are clearly strengths women wish to retain in their exercise of power. At the same time, they need to work toward greater wholeness by developing other dimensions of power.

While retaining their skills for empowering others, women need to develop self-determination, the practical abilities to influence life on all levels. Many women are better at empowering others than they are at self-empowerment. Exerting direct influence on events may be a new experience for them, but it need not mean giving up the other kinds of interaction which they value. It helps if they can see women who embody wholeness in the exercise of this kind of power.

As they sort through their own relationships to power, women search for mentors. They look for women who embody the kind of courage and risk-taking required for decisive public action. Stories of these women fire our imaginations and open up possibilities. Sharing such stories in spiritual direction is a way of creating alternatives. Truth conveyed in narrative invites us to enter into the story and make our own judgment or decision as a result.

One woman whose story creates possibilities for Christian women is Catherine of Siena. A young woman said of her attraction to Catherine.

> She shows me that the way to change things is to grow into my full self and from my personal power base DO what I feel called to do.

Catherine's life underscores the fact that holiness is power.[8] The fourteenth century world in which Catherine lived, with its disputed papal elections and chaotic claims of two popes, its simony, greed, and neglect of the poor, provided ample reason to despair of the uses of power and to distance oneself from its exercise. Catherine, however, became a powerful and effective reformer. Her life illustrates the close link between contemplation and social consciousness. She fearlessly confronted the religious and secular institutions of her time, castigating senators, popes and kings for their abuse of power and unjust treatment of the poor. Her power was rooted in her union with God. In one of her letters, she writes:

> Fear and serve God, with no regard to thyself; and then do not care for what people may say, except to have compassion on them . . . if it shall be for His honor and thy salvation, He will send thee means and the way when thou art thinking nothing about it, in a way that thou wouldst never have imagined.[9]

A life centered in God gives one the kind of assurance and imagination needed to risk challenging unjust political systems. Sanctity is itself powerful.

Another woman who models a similar wholeness in her use of power is Dorothy Day. While Catherine chose celibacy as a space of freedom for her exercise of power, Dorothy was a single parent whose daughter Tamar Teresa was a source of great joy and gratitude. At one point Dorothy struggled to raise Tamar alone on the unpredictable wages of a free-lance writer. Like many single mothers today, she seemed to be trying to survive far from the centers of political power.

However, Dorothy was a major figure in twentieth century America. By the end of her life her Catholic Worker Movement enjoyed a vast influence. When she died in 1980 at the
age of eighty-three, the historian David O'Brien called her "the
most significant, interesting, and influential person in the history of American Catholicism."[10] A central element of Dorothy's spirituality was belief in the Body of Christ, a conviction
that each act of love contributes to the balance of love in the
world and that each act of strength and courage, no matter how
small, changes the world.

Dorothy challenged and resisted the institutional forces
that lead to poverty and war. While marching on picket lines
or in jail, she was able to ignore criticism and rejection because
she held herself accountable to God's word. "Too much
praise," she once observed, "makes you feel you must be doing
something terribly wrong." Holiness was the basis of her
power, but she was no saint in the traditional mold. "Don't
call me a saint," she once said. "I don't want to be dismissed
that easily." Hers was a troubling kind of saintliness, one not
easily domesticated. What strikes us about it is the way in
which she combined free, courageous action with compassion
for the poor. She had achieved the kind of inner freedom which
enabled her to use her powers in strong and effective ways.

The poet and novelist, May Sarton, reflects on this same
truth in her journal, *At Seventy*. She tells of a series of readings
she gave at Hartford College in Connecticut, a series she called
"The Seasons of Womanhood." In the course of her talk she
had remarked, "This is the best time of my life. I love being
old." At that point someone in the audience asked, "Why is it
good to be old?" Sarton says that she answered spontaneously
and a bit defensively since she sensed incredulity on the part
of the questioner:

> Because I am more myself than I have ever been.
> There is less conflict. I am happier, more balanced,
> and (I heard myself say rather aggressively) more pow-
> erful. I felt it was rather an odd word, "powerful", but
> I think it is true. It might have been more accurate to
> say "I am better able to use my powers." I am surer of

144

what my life is all about, have less self-doubt to con-
quer. . . . [11]

This sense of personal power comes, as Sarton suggests, with
deeper knowledge of who we are and what we value, along
with a conviction of our intrinsic worth. This may take years
to develop, but when it is in place, it changes all of a woman's
relationships.

What these three women convey in different ways is the
fact that it is possible to be both assertive and caring. Power
comes from combining integrity and truth with compassion
and concern for others. From a base of holiness, women such
as Catherine of Siena and Dorothy Day have exerted influence
on history and society, in the public as well as the private
sphere. They model alternative forms of power which are not
based on polarization and dichotomy but which affirm mu
tuality and the importance of making the world different.

DEVELOPING STRATEGIES FOR CHANGE

In her fine book, *Powers of the Weak*, Elizabeth Janeway
analyzes the role those in subordinate positions, especially
women, play in the reform of social power. Janeway defines the
weak as those in lesser social positions.[12] Those in stronger positions succeed, she says, because the weak accept the current
definitions of how things are. The strong, those in leadership
positions, benefit from conventional arrangements and are not
likely to undertake a shift in the structures of power. That is
the task of the weak.

Janeway describes three powers of the weak. We might
also see her project as a practical agenda for implementing relational power, for exercising the kind of influence that will
help to restore mutuality to power interactions.

1. Disbelief

The first power of the weak is the use of the ordered power
to disbelieve. It is the refusal to accept the definition of oneself—as laity, woman, gay, or black—which is put forward by

the powerful. The power to define is often exercised in a stereotypical way and reflects the view of life of the powerful: blacks are less intelligent than whites, women are ruled by emotions, gay persons suffer from a psychological aberration. Defining also involves the assignment of acceptable roles to subordinate groups, usually forms of service which the dominant group cannot or does not want to do for itself. So, for example, women cannot be ordained in some denominations, but they can perform other tasks necessary for the running of a parish. They are not suited to holding public office, but they can be entrusted with the well-being of children and the family.

Those in subordinate positions grant legitimacy, or give authority, to social arrangements by accepting current definitions and uses of power. The first power the weak can exercise is therefore to refuse to believe that the way things are is the way they are supposed to be. A woman describes such a change in herself.

> I see myself right now as a daughter, as a woman, being called in some way to speak God's dreams, speak God's hopes for the world to those who most long to hear it. I see myself called by God to stand tall in my truth, to speak the word only I have to bear. I sense God prodding me, encouraging me, laying hands on me to do this, and also preparing me, purifying my heart for the task, and helping me painfully to live out of my truest self.

Disbelief is the beginning of liberation. It is the first step toward imagining alternatives.

2. Coming Together

Coming together is especially important for women, since our lives have often separated us not only from the world of action, but from one another. However, there is power in circles of women, base communities, gatherings of the laity, and other groups who join together for support and encouragement. When Janeway designates coming together as a power of the weak, she is speaking, of course, as a social analyst, not from a religious perspective. Her perspective can be integrated, however, with testimony regarding the faith dimension of such gatherings. Women experience the Spirit in their midst as they gather in such groups.

An important function of coming together, whether in groups or with another woman, is to help women deal with the conflict and distress that is generated by their new perceptions of the truth about themselves and the world. As psychological studies show, these more truthful conceptions are bound to come into opposition with the views they have absorbed from the dominant groups, whether that be church, husbands, or men in general. They need confirmation and support.

3. Acting in Common Pursuit of Shared Goals

Direct action may feel foreign and dangerous to women who believe that politics, like power, is tainted with evil. Janeway addresses this reluctance to engage in political action.

> There's no way to stop the world and get off; we're all here together, both those who shun power and those who lust after it. Whether the weak intervene or not, they are touched by the continuing dynamics of the political process. The input that they don't supply is not just lost; its absence allows other considerations to weigh more heavily and to unbalance the relationship. Reject the chance to act for your own good and the world will still trundle on, but it will do so according to the demands of other people.[13]

Such considerations are especially helpful when women are discerning action for justice, or when they experience the sinfulness of the very groups dedicated to such causes. A sister, for example, who had joined with a group of other women to work for peace in Central America, was discouraged by the group's inability to deal with its own power conflicts. She struggled with her desire to withdraw from the group because

147

all the members seemed so mired in their own human limitations. It was difficult for her to commit herself to healing the power relationships within the group itself, but she saw that such a commitment was integral to her desire to work for justice.

Murphy Davis, an ordained Presbyterian minister, speaks of her willingness to sustain the discouragement experienced in direct action for justice. The founder of the Atlanta branch of Southern Prison Ministry, Davis persists in her efforts to work with prisoners and their families in spite of the obstacles created by prison authorities. She finds the story of the widow and the judge in Luke 18 confirming for her ministry. The judge cared nothing for God and had no regard for human beings. But it was expedient for him to give the widow her rights or wear out. "We have to go back and go back and go back and make a nuisance of ourselves," Davis says, "or we'll never accomplish anything."[14]

This focus on direct action brings our reflections on the place of power in women's spirituality full circle. We began with definitions of power and women's contributions to the meaning of power. Spiritual guidance must take seriously contemporary women's need and struggle to understand and exercise power.

FOR PRAYER AND REFLECTION

1. Power in Your Life: A Reflection Exercise

Reflect on the following questions, and record your thoughts in your journal, if you wish.

a. What are the images and emotions that first come to mind when you think of power? How is/was power exercised by the influential women and men in your life, i.e., mother, father, teachers, religious leaders? Can you name any women who have exercised power in holistic ways, i.e., both giving and receiving, influencing and being influenced?

148

b. Make a metaphor for power.

c. Are you powerful or weak? In what ways?

d. What experiences of your power have been most satisfying to you?

e. In what areas of your life would you like to exercise more influence? What prevents you from doing so? How can you change this?

2. Women Leaders: A Meditation

Early Christian women saw themselves as freed by the Spirit to become founders and leaders of house churches. Yet their contributions have usually been ignored.

Read about and meditate on some of these women:

a.	Lydia of Thyatira	Acts 16:14
b.	Prisca and Aquila	1 Corinthians 16:19
		Romans 16:3–5
		2 Timothy 4:19
		Acts 18:1–3, 18–19, 26
c.	Phoebe	Romans 16:1–2

3. Blessings

Blessings, especially those which include oil for healing, are an important ritual for affirming and strengthening women's power. One young woman describes their significance in a women's group: "We pray for each other and anoint each other with whatever words have not been said or been said often. It is such a powerful time and a time of bonding." The following are some blessings, or you may want to create your own.

While laying hands on the other person: "May the God of Judith, Deborah, and Ruth strengthen you to speak and act in her name."

While anointing hands and head with oil: "Our God is a God of wholeness. By this anointing may you be healed of your fears and fragmentation. May your communion with the divine Spirit empower you to act on behalf of justice and truth."

149

4. A Litany of Women's Power

All: Spirit of Life, we remember today the women, named and unnamed, who throughout time have used the power and gifts you gave them to change the world. We call upon these foremothers to help us discover within ourselves your power— and the ways to use it to bring about the Kingdom of Justice and Peace.

We remember SARAH who with Abraham answered God's call to forsake her homeland and put their faith in a covenant with the Lord.
We pray for her power of faith.

We remember ESTHER and DEBORAH, who by acts of individual courage saved their nation.
We pray for their power of courage to act for the greater good.

We remember MARY MAGDALENE, and the other women who followed Jesus who were not believed when they announced the resurrection.
We pray for their power of belief in the face of skepticism.

We remember PHOEBE, PRISCILLA, and the other women leaders of the early church.
We pray for their power to spread the Gospel and inspire congregations.

We remember the Abbesses of the Middle Ages who kept faith and knowledge alive.
We pray for their power of leadership.

We remember TERESA of Avila and CATHERINE of Siena who challenged the corruption of the church during the Renaissance.
We pray for their powers of intelligence and outspokenness. (At this point you may wish to remember contemporary women, and their contributions, from your culture).

All: We remember our own mothers and grandmothers whose lives shaped ours.
We pray for the special power they attempted to pass on to us.

We pray for the women who are victims of violence in their homes.

May they be granted the power to overcome fear and seek solutions.

We pray for those women who face a life of poverty and malnutrition. May they be granted the power of hopefulness to work together for a better life.

We pray for the women today who are "firsts" in their fields.

May they be granted the power to persevere and open up new possibilities for all women.

All: We pray for our daughters and granddaughters. May they be granted the power to seek that life which is uniquely theirs.

(HERE, add any women you would like to remember or for whom you wish to pray)

All: We have celebrated the power of many women past and present. It is time now to celebrate ourselves. Within each of us is that same life and light and love. Within each of us lie the seeds of power and glory. Our bodies can touch with love; our hearts can heal; our minds can seek out faith and truth and justice. Spirit of Life, be with us in our quest. Amen.

(This litany is from Ann M. Heidkamp, *No Longer Strangers. A Resource for Women and Worship,* edited by Iben Gjerding and Katherine Kinnamon, Geneva, WCC Publications, 1983, pp. 24–25).

[1]"Women and Power," *Work in Progress* (Wellesley, MA: Stone Center for Developmental Services and Studies, 1982), pp. 1–2.

[2]For further discussion of these developments, see Janet O. Hagberg, *Real Power. The Stages of Personal Power in Organizations* (Minneapolis: Winston Press, 1984); Letty M. Russell, *Growth in Partnership* (Philadelphia: Westminster Press, 1981) and *Household of Freedom*; Bernard Loomer, "Two Kinds of Power," in *Criterion: Journal of the University of Chicago Divinity School* (Winter 1976), 11–29; James D. Whitehead and Evelyn Eaton Whitehead, *The Emerging Laity. Returning Leadership to the Community of Faith* (New York: Doubleday, 1986).

[3]Pp. 54–55.

[4]*Women's Ways of Knowing*, p. 173.

[5]Joe Peacock, "Politics of Whimsy at Greenham Common," in *Sojourners* 12 (February 1983), 8–10.

[6]See Jean Baker Miller, *Toward a New Psychology of Women* (Boston: Beacon Press, 1976), p. 124.

[7]Quoted in the Cambridge Women's Peace Collective, *My Country Is the Whole World. An Anthology of Women's Work on Peace and War* (London: Pandora Press, 1984), p. 254.

[8]See Eleanor McLaughlin, "Women, Power and the Pursuit of Holiness in Medieval Christianity," in *Women of Spirit. Female Leadership in the Jewish and Christian Traditions*, ed. Rosemary Ruether and Eleanor McLaughlin (New York: Simon & Schuster, 1979), pp. 99–130; Carola Parks, OP, "Social and Political Consciousness in the Letters of Catherine of Siena," in *Western Spirituality. Historical Roots, Ecumenical Routes*, ed. Matthew Fox (Santa Fe, NM: Bear & Company, 1981), pp. 249–260.

[9]*Women of Spirit*, p. 118.

[10]"The Pilgrimage of Dorothy Day," *Commonweal* (December 19, 1980), 711.

[11](New York: W.W. Norton & Company, 1984), p. 10.

[12](New York: Alfred A. Knopf, 1980).

[13]*Powers of the Weak*, pp. 14–15.

[14]Quoted by Joyce Hollyday in "Community with Homeless People and Prisoners: An Open Door in Atlanta," *The Rise of Christian Conscience*, ed. Jim Wallis (San Francisco: Harper & Row, 1987), p. 85.

8

Violence Against Women:
The Spiritual Dimension

Books on spiritual direction seldom talk
about violence against women. Yet large numbers of women
have personal experience of sexual and domestic violence.
Even conservative estimates indicate how widespread such violence is. Wife battering, rape, incest, and child abuse cut
across all class, religious, and color lines. Ntozake Shange conveys the magnitude of the problem in her poem, "With No Immediate Cause":

> every 3 minutes a woman is beaten
> every 5 minutes a
> woman is raped/every ten minutes
> a little girl is molested[1]

Statistics on the extent of such violence only scratch the surface, and do not include all the violence that goes unreported,
or forms of violence such as verbal abuse on the street, tele-
phone harassment, and degrading media portrayals of women.
Nor do statistics reflect the psychological abuse—criticisms,
threats, humiliations—that occurs in relationships. Even for

women who have so far not experienced it directly, the reality of sexual and domestic violence creates a climate of vulnerability and fear that all women must live with daily, a climate affecting all our relationships.

The topic of violence may surface in the spiritual direction context in any number of ways. Sometimes an experience in prayer, a movie, or a present relationship will trigger a long-buried memory of abuse. At times a session of storytelling with other women either evokes memories or finally provides a safe setting for recalling childhood abuse. I have also had women in spiritual direction who had already been through extensive therapy to heal the pain of wife battering or physical assault, but who were still dealing with dimensions of these experiences many years later. In other cases the violence is an immediate and current issue, as it was for one young woman who came to a spiritual direction session terribly shaken by the frightening and harassing phone calls she had been getting from a man who was a casual acquaintance.

While issues related to violence may surface in many ways in spiritual direction, they may also fail to arise for a number of reasons. It takes time for women even to realize and remember some forms of violence; violence against women has been taken for granted by our culture for so long that women themselves have taken it for granted. Women may not be aware that it has an impact on their spirituality. They may carry a sense of shame and guilt about an experience that makes them fearful that rejection and judgment will result if they reveal it. A spiritual director's lack of awareness or denial of the pervasiveness of sexual and domestic violence sometimes prevents the director from listening well when a woman alludes to the topic. We miss what she is trying to say, or inadvertently deliver the message that such incidents are not really important, or are too delicate to talk about. The fact is they are extremely important because of the deep and lasting impact they have made, and they must be talked about if the woman is to be healed.

The reality of violence strongly influences our spirituality as women. As the silence surrounding this issue continues to lift, more of us will be exploring the religious dimensions of violence in spiritual direction.² In this chapter we will look first at some of the issues which violence raises, and then at some paths to healing which spiritual direction can facilitate. A final section will examine nonviolence as an option for women.

Sexual and domestic violence has a profound effect on a woman's relationship with herself, with others, and with God. Since all three relationships are central to her spirituality, it is important to understand the religious issues inherent in each.

1. Feelings of Shame and Guilt

A woman who planned to tell her spiritual director that she was sexually abused by her brother when she was a child arrived at the session with a bouquet of flowers. She was feeling such shame and guilt that she feared her spiritual director would almost certainly reject her once he knew the truth about her. Women are accustomed to bearing responsibility for relationships. When violence occurs, their first response may be to wonder what they did to bring it about. Feelings of shame often prevent them from even talking about it.

A sister who was raped, in trying to tell her community how they might be helpful in such instances, describes a rape victim's reaction.

> Almost immediately she feels a sense of guilt. The guilt is her irrational way of asserting that of course she did have *some* power—so she must have had *some* responsibility. No matter how incapable the woman is to prevent the experience, she almost inevitably feels that she should somehow have prevented it. The guilt is like a refrain that replays in her mind, "I'm sorry, I'm sorry." She may not be able to tell anyone why, or even that the feelings of guilt are present. A religious woman probably knows how irrational they

are. But they are one more aspect of powerlessness: a thought pattern over which she has no control.[3]

This tendency to feel responsible is reinforced by our cultural pattern of blaming the victim. This is often the attitude of police departments. It is also very much alive in the churches, where the implied or explicit question is, "What did she do to cause it?"

The experience of shame and guilt takes many forms in the lives of women who experience violence. Looking back on an experience of child abuse, for example, they may now think that they should have known what was happening or how to stop it. Women who experience sexual harassment from men in work situations wonder if they are too warm and friendly, or if they are dressed too attractively.

These feelings of shame and guilt may be accompanied by intense anger and then discomfort with the anger. The anger can increase her feelings of guilt if a woman believes that her Christian faith calls on her to forgive her enemy, and she cannot bring herself to forgive the person who has injured her so. In her book on *Battered Wives*, Del Martin shares a letter from a battered wife who describes her efforts to seek help.

> I did. Early in our marriage I went to a clergyman who, after a few visits, told me that my husband meant no real harm, that he was just confused and felt insecure. I was encouraged to be more tolerant and understanding. Most important, I was told to forgive him the beatings just as Christ had forgiven me from the cross. I did that, too.[4]

Christian teachings on forgiveness can increase the emotional pain of survivors of violence unless it is made clear that forgiveness does not mean allowing things to go on as before. Since forgiveness is not a solitary action but a gesture of grace in relationships, the shape it takes often depends on justice being enacted against the offender, and evidence of repentance on the part of the person who has injured the woman. This is

157

presupposed when Marie Fortune describes what the act of forgiveness finally means.

> I will no longer allow this experience to dominate my life. I will not let it continue to make me feel bad about myself. I will not let it limit my ability to love and trust others in my life. I will not let my memory of the experience continue to victimize and control me.[5]

Such an approach allows us to move beyond the pain and make a new beginning.

2. Violated Integrity

Experiences of violence damage a woman's sense of physical and spiritual integrity. Her body has been invaded against her will, used as an object by another, or injured by someone she trusted to care for her. She may have feelings of being unclean or needing to wash. She often feels worthless and used. Because of our body/spirit unity, violence is a deep violation of a woman's personal integrity or wholeness. She knows firsthand how fragile her person and her world are.

> This sense that violence and violation disturb the order of the universe is also inherent in the archaic meaning of these words, which define them as "desecration". These ancient meanings need to be brought more forcefully before our "modern" minds as we consider rape as a spiritual crisis: The experience of victims suggests that the integrity of the body is sacred. Rape demeans precisely that which we ought most fully to cherish.[6]

The approach to healing must seek to restore a woman's feelings of wholeness and of control over her own person and life.

Violence not only affects personal integrity; it takes a terrible toll on our ability to relate to others. It threatens a woman's sense that she is lovable and can ever be loved. Moreover, being so betrayed in a relationship with someone she knows makes it very difficult for a woman to trust others, especially men. She experiences the world and relationships with others as radically unsafe. It takes a long time to work through these fears.

3. A Crisis of Faith and Trust in God

One of the contributors to *I Never Told Anyone. Writings by Women Survivors of Child Sexual Abuse* prefaces her account by saying that if she could give another title to her story, it would be "Why?"[7] Violence is an encounter with the power of evil in the world. Such suffering is not random or abstract, but an experience of evil directed against our person. It threatens a woman's trust in God and raises many faith questions: Was this somehow God's will? Where was God when I was so in need? How could God love me and let me go through this? Is this suffering a punishment for the sinfulness in my life? What kind of a world is this? Answering these questions on a personal level is part of healing. It means moving from feeling abandoned and alone to a sense of God's spirit with us.

Rape, battering, and child sexual abuse are life-threatening, death-dealing experiences. Women who go through them fear for their physical safety and feel they may die. Even when the threat of physical death is not immediate, survivors of such experiences find parts of themselves closing off or dying. Such encounters with loss and death create great grief, and the healing experience is in most of its dimensions one of grieving. There may be dreams and flashbacks of the experience, a mixture of strong emotions, and anger at God for allowing such a thing to happen. A betrayal of trust is experienced in the relationship with God as well as in other relationships.

PATHS TO HEALING

We have looked briefly at some of the spiritual dimensions of sexual and domestic violence. While keeping in mind the fact that each woman's situation will be different, there are a number of ways in which spiritual companions can support the healing process.

1. Listening with Love

This is, of course, what spiritual friendship is all about. Yet it needs to be emphasized again in relation to women and violence. One of the principal ways in which spiritual companions assist the healing process is by being present to the person in her pain, listening to her story, and offering her unqualified love and acceptance. Survivors of sex abuse may need repeated assurances that they are not guilty; they were victimized. Likewise, battered women need reassurance that they did not deserve the beatings, even if they did something their partner did not like; that is no excuse for the beatings. Such love and listening affirms again the woman's worth and value, and helps her regain a sense of her own identity and power. It provides her with a supportive presence while she develops her own strength.

A spiritual companion can also help by expressing her personal outrage at the suffering the woman has experienced, as well as her fears in face of the potential for such violence in her own life. Honest recognition of our common vulnerability lessens a woman's sense that she is isolated and set apart by her experience of violence. A very effective form of spiritual companionship is found, for example, in shelters for battered women where they can gather around a kitchen table for coffee and tell their stories to one another. They gather new strength from common courage and find their humanity affirmed by women who have known similar pain.

The spiritual direction relationship itself is key here. By providing consistent, non-judgmental caring, an individual or group enables a woman to rebuild her capacity for trust. One young woman was in spiritual direction several years after being badly beaten by her husband. The experience had left her doubting that she could ever love or be loved again. Telling her story and being affirmed in her goodness was an important aspect of her healing process. It supported her in her struggle to reconstitute her world and her relationships.

2. Exploring the Religious Issues

Help for the religious crisis created by experiences of violence does not consist *primarily* in providing theological answers, although these can be useful and freeing. It lies rather in accompanying the woman through the death/resurrection passage to her own answers. Spiritual guides are there to facilitate the process as God brings about healing. Nevertheless, along the way we may suggest resources for prayer or reflection, or provide alternative ways of viewing theological truths. The healing process should bring a deepening conviction for the woman that God is on her side and the side of life and wholeness, not on the side of the violence.

In "Where Was God?" Louise Garrison describes how in her journey of healing from the experience of incest she gradually found her way through feelings of being abandoned by God. She says that she had searched her soul in its depths for an answer to the question, "Where was God when I needed God most?" In that search she found, she says, a new freedom that comes from experiencing God.

> I have found the answer. My answer came from the crucified Christ as he cried out in his passion from the cross, "Eloi, Eloi, lama sabachthani?" "My God, my God, why hast thou forsaken me?" Surely a God who has such mercy and such love would not let a son die on the cross, even if we are sinners. I, a mere mortal, with limited capabilities for love, would move heaven and earth and fight with all my being for the life of my son. If God's love is greater than ours, why wasn't the son saved?
>
> Scripture tells us in Matthew 27:40 that the chief priests, lawyers, and elders asked the same question. Even the bandits who were crucified with him taunted him in the same way. Jesus died a broken man—mocked by his accusers, betrayed by his disciple, and denied by one of his closest friends. Jeered at, spit at, taunted, ridiculed, and laughed at. But God had the last word, because Jesus overcame every

earthly affliction. No matter what the abuse, the message God has given us in the resurrection is that coer-
cive power never works; it only destroys. God has the
final word, and that word is Life.[8]

In struggling to answer questions such as Garrison's "Where
was God?" it is helpful to reflect with the person on God's relationship to evil. It is not God who sends us suffering, even
for our good. But God cannot prevent all evil in a world of free
agents. When tragedy strikes, we find the presence and activity
of God grieving with us in the pain and working with us to try
to redeem it.

Another woman told me about a similar experience in
coming to the realization that God could be a force for healing
and hope in her life.

> I was the victim of sexual abuse in my family growing
> up. I did not deal with this and after nineteen years of
> stuffing [my emotions] I was diagnosed with cancer of
> the cervix. I began to seek help for the pain in my
> heart. Slowly, inch by inch, I began to let the pain out
> and God in.
>
> After healing prayer and conversion I went to an
> assault center for women molested as children. In
> prayer the day of going to the center I heard Isaiah 54
> in my mind: "Do not be afraid, you will not be put to
> shame, do not be dismayed, you will not be disgraced;
> for you will forget the shame of your youth." My God
> had spoken to me, gifting me with this passage. There-
> fore, there is a God who *is* good and wants me healed.

What is at stake in the experience of violence is not so much
abstract ideas about God, but trust in a relationship with God.
Inadequate notions of God's will and of God's relation to evil
and suffering can block this relationship, and it is helpful to
clear them away. But finally it is a matter of helping the
woman find the existential answer, as Job did, in an experience
of God's healing presence. Healing the wounds of violence is
a resurrection experience. The wounds remain, but they can

be transformed into a new kind of wholeness as a woman discovers new strengths within herself and her relationships.

3. Suggesting New Ways of Reading Biblical Passages

Women with violent partners may believe that the bible supports the subordinate position of women in the family and decrees that a wife be subject to her husband. How can they free themselves from such situations and still feel they are being true to what the bible commands? They need help in seeing that the bible is on their side and does not support battering and violence against women. Unfortunately, they may have heard from pulpits and bible groups that the husband is the head of the household and the wife's duty is to submit and obey. The inferior position of women in the family is presented as divinely ordained.

Passages frequently used to reinforce such a view are the Genesis depictions of creation and the fall, and sections of epistles such as 1 Timothy 2:12–14 and 1 Corinthians 11:8. Ephesians 5:22–24 is an especially influential passage, made all the more so by its frequent inclusion in the marriage liturgy itself.

> Wives should regard their husbands as they regard the Lord, since as Christ is head of the Church and saves the whole body, so is a husband the head of his wife. As the Church submits to Christ, so wives should submit to their husbands in everything.

Such readings make the subjection of a woman to her husband seem just and sacred. Her duty is to bear with him in patience. For Catholic women, this is reinforced by the prohibition against divorce, which leads to a belief that marriage and the family should be preserved at all costs.

Learning to see these biblical passages in a new way is part of the healing process for battered women.[9] There are several aspects to this new reading:

a. Situating these writings in their cultural context. This means accepting the human authorship and cul-

163

tural conditioning of the bible. Elisabeth Fiorenza has shown, for example, that the prescriptions for domestic order found in Colossians 3:18–25, 1 Peter 2:11–3:12, and Ephesians 5:21–33 are based on the patriarchal arrangements found in late first century Greco-Roman households with their hierarchy of husband, wife, children, slaves. In order to reduce tensions between Christians and pagan society, the authors of these epistles advocate adopting this patriarchal order, even though such subordination is at variance with Jesus' vision of community, which is founded on a discipleship of equals.[10]

b. *Highlighting biblical passages which call for mutual love, respect, and care.* The Song of Songs conveys a vision of relationships in which there is mutual love and respect between woman and man. Galatians 3:28 declares that in the Christian community there is a new pattern of relationships, where differences are no longer to lead to dominance and subordination, as they do in patriarchal marriage.

> All baptized in Christ, you have all clothed yourselves in Christ, and there are no more distinctions between Jew and Greek, slave and free, male and female, but you are all one in Christ Jesus.

This concern for the full dignity of persons applies to male and female relationships, and calls for mutual love and respect in marriage.

c. *Sharing the results of current research on problematic passages.* Such study has been especially helpful with the Genesis stories. It shows, for example, that the creation account in Genesis 1 implies no inferiority of woman. God creates humanity immediately as male and female.

> God said, "Let us make humanity in our own image, in the likeness of ourselves, and let them be masters of the fish of the sea." . . . God created humanity in

164

the image of himself, in the image of God he created
it, male and female he created them (Gen 1:26–27).

The creation story in Genesis 2 has come down to us as the
Adam and Eve story, with its image of woman coming from
man's rib and its overtones of male superiority. Phyllis Trible
has done a penetrating analysis of this story in which she
shows that the relationship of this first couple is actually one
of mutuality and equality, not one of female subordination.
Both originate from God, and are given to one another as equal
partners.[11]

Other sections of the bible may need to be discussed with
battered women. Their importance depends on the power they
have in a woman's faith life. Approaching key biblical passages
in a new way assures a woman in a battering situation that she
can preserve her faith and yet take the action she needs to protect and heal herself and her family.

4. Assisting with Cleansing and Healing Rituals

Women turn to rituals to help them with the long and
painful process of recovery from violence. Because ritual
reaches us on all levels, it touches our emotions and restores
a sense of bodily integrity. It is also a way of making tangible
the support of a faith community. Moreover, ritual allows us
to reclaim a time and space that have been taken from us by
the experience of violence.

For all these reasons, women choose to have some kind of
celebration or ritual on the anniversary of the event. One
woman was assaulted in the kitchen of her home. Each year on
that date she invites a group of friends to celebrate a kitchen
supper with her. Another woman marks the date with a ceremony of lighting candles and praying with friends as a way of
continuing to ward off the darkness and affirm the greater
power of light in her life. In *Sexual Violence. The Unmentionable Sin*, Marie Fortune gives several helpful examples of the
role of ritual in facilitating the healing process. One is a very
simple ritual of cleansing.

> A woman who had been raped realized that she felt somehow stained by the assault. It was not that she felt dirty or stigmatized by the sexual contact *per se.* Rather, in the violation of her person, she felt that something had been put on her which she could not cast off. So she decided that she wanted to experience some form of ritual cleansing in order to be cleansed of the violation. She sought the help of a woman minister friend who suggested that she gather her close friends and then use water to wash away the stain of violation.[12]

Like the minister in this account, spiritual friends may be called on to help create a ritual or to be present at one. Reflecting in the context of spiritual direction on the symbols and actions she wishes to make a part of the ritual is one way for a woman to clarify the meaning the experience holds for her. Women may also want to create a ritual to express their solidarity with the victims of violence throughout the world, or to express the pain that comes from living with the many forms of indirect violence and the constant threat of violence.

5. Healing of Memories

For some women it is helpful to do guided work in the healing of memories around experiences of violence. Women are usually not helped by this if the experience is a recent one, or if the emotional pain is still very strong and is being explored for the first time. It can, however, help with memories of long standing which have been dealt with in therapy but still continue to interfere with a woman's present peace and prayer. Women generally know quite instinctively whether such an approach is well timed and appropriate for what they are going through.

Such healing work has three steps.

a. The woman is helped to relax through deep breathing or other guided exercises.

b. The spiritual director invites her to return to the memory, entering into the scene again, along with the feelings it

166

produced. Then she is invited to have Jesus or another healing figure come upon the scene. The woman watches what the healing figure does, listens to what he or she says, and interacts as she feels moved while the experience unfolds. She can do all this in the privacy of her inner space, or she can share the experience step by step with her director as it unfolds. The latter approach enables the director to offer occasional suggestions, such as: "Just stay there a few moments, really taking that (good experience) in"; or "Tell Jesus (or the healing figure) about the fear or distress you are feeling and see what he says." Some women prefer that the healer be a woman, such as Mary of Nazareth or Mary Magdalene, rather than Jesus. This gives them a greater sense of comfort and understanding.

c. The woman and the director process the experience after its conclusion, exploring its meanings. This tells them, among other things, whether the work is done or should be repeated again next meeting. If the woman has had a profound religious experience, the director can suggest that she keep bringing it back into her prayer in the weeks to follow.

6. Providing Referrals and Practical Support

If a spiritual companion is the person a woman trusts most, she may break through her fear and talk for the first time with this person about the violence she is now experiencing or has experienced in the past. Depending on the situation, she may need immediate help to protect herself and assure her safety and that of her children. This may mean calling the police or a crisis line. She may also need therapy or a support group. In such instances the spiritual director needs to know how to call on the resources of the community, how to refer the woman to specialists who have the kind of expertise she needs. This means that spiritual directors need to investigate and have information on hand on the resources available in their areas.

7. Working Against Violence Toward Women

In earlier chapters I have described spiritual direction as a prophetic ministry. As such, it involves a commitment to making God's promise of wholeness and liberation a reality. Women who have survived violence themselves often choose to become actively involved in the struggle to end violence: marching in demonstrations such as Women Take Back the Night; leading groups for battered or abused women; working for education programs in churches.

Spiritual guides must also be committed to making the world a safer place for women. They do this by refusing to perpetuate the dominance/submission model of relationships and by pressing for new roles, structures and symbol systems for male/female relationships. They may find other ways, too, to help end the cycle of violence in human life.

NONVIOLENCE AND WOMEN

Many Christian women are drawn to nonviolence as a means of bringing about social change. As these women grow in their awareness of women's issues, they may need to integrate this feminist consciousness with their commitment to nonviolence.[13] Spiritual direction can be a good setting for doing this. This process of integration can be framed in terms of two questions.

1. *How can we bring about a new world without using violence ourselves?*

While women want to discard their traditional passivity, they do not want to adopt traditional male violence. A central conviction of feminism is that all forms of violence and oppression are interrelated. This conviction is based on a recognition of the fundamental interconnectedness of all of life and a rejection of the principle of domination and subjugation. War, racism, and sexism are all part of the same fabric of violence. Hence women in the peace movement are disturbed when a hierarchy of kinds of violence is established, and women's concerns are considered less important than other forms of violence. Work for peace cannot ignore the threat of violence aimed at women on a daily basis. The elimination of any form of violence weakens its hold on all other areas.

Nonviolence is a way of transforming relationships. This

is due in great part to its power to simultaneously accept and reject; it enables us to acknowledge and connect with what is valuable in a person while at the same time resisting and challenging a person's oppressive attitudes and behavior. As Barbara Deming says,

> In this form of struggle we address ourselves both to that which we refuse to accept from others and that which we have in common with them—however much or little that may be.[14]

Gandhi's program for nonviolence included both "ahimsa"—action based on the refusal to do harm, because we love and respect the personhood of the enemy—and "noncooperation"—action based on the belief that power is kept in place by cooperation and can be broken by the refusal of persons to be subjected any longer. Theories of nonviolence help women find a way to offer respect for persons while at the same time refusing to cooperate in injustice. We can be angry while refusing to destroy.

2. *How do we advocate nonviolence without lapsing into a weak passivity?*

The stereotype of women is that they are passive and weak, while men are active and strong. Women therefore fear that nonviolence may be too well suited to them, and may perpetuate this stereotype. In light of this danger, a woman's commitment to non-violence must be based on a rejection of passivity and a strong sense of her own value as a human being. Nonviolence, as those who are students of Gandhi know, is not a submissive or passive attitude toward oppression and violence. It is an attitude of resistance to oppression and a commitment to the struggle for freedom for oneself and all others. Gandhi's term "satyagraha" means truth force. It implies an assertive, positive stand, one which relies on the strength of truth rather than on physical force.

Training in nonviolence must be grounded in spiritual development and empowerment of the self. When a person is so empowered, she will not accept her own degradation or that of others. Women find that they can live out their commitment to nonviolence better when they know how to stand up for and defend themselves, and when they are able to affirm their own feeling, thinking, and speaking. In this way they can both maintain respect and extend it to others.

I hope these reflections on issues of violence and nonviolence have confirmed their importance for women's spirituality today. As the silence surrounding sexual and domestic violence continues to lift, more women will be exploring its spiritual dimensions in spiritual direction. This in turn will expand our future understanding of the role spiritual friendship can play in healing the effects of such violence.

FOR PRAYER AND REFLECTION

1. Self-Blessing

Gather together a white candle, a small bowl or cup of water and a stick of incense. Pick a quiet time and space. Light the candle and incense and sit quietly, letting all tension slip away and all worried thought leave your body/mind.

Dip your fingers in the water and touch your eyes saying, "Bless my eyes that I may have clarity of vision."

Dip your fingers in the water and touch your mouth saying, "Bless my mouth that I may speak the truth."

Dip your fingers in the water and touch your ears saying, "Bless my ears that I may hear all that is spoken unto me."

Dip your fingers in the water and touch your heart saying, "Bless my heart that I may be filled with love."

Dip your fingers in the water and touch your womb saying, "Bless my womb that I may be in touch with my creative energies and the creative energy of the universe."

Dip your fingers in the water and touch your feet saying, "Bless my feet that I may find and walk on my own true path."

Quietly reflect on the words you have spoken and feel yourself filled with a peaceful, loving energy.

When you feel complete, put out the candle. Empty the bowl and wash it carefully.

(This exercise is from Diane Mariechild, *Mother Wit. A Feminist Guide to Psychic Development*, Freedom, CA: The Crossing Press, 1982, p. 146.)

2. A Meditation on the Self as Temple of God

In 1 Corinthians 3:16–17, Paul says:

Do you not know that you are God's temple and that
God's Spirit dwells in you?
Whoever destroys God's temple, God will destroy.
For God's temple is holy, and you are that temple.

The meaning of this passage is deepened by this statement found in Jennifer Baker Fleming's book, *Stopping Wife Abuse*.

You have both the freedom and the responsibility to care about yourself. You have the right to think and feel and make choices and changes. Consider thinking about yourself in new ways:

I am not to blame for being beaten and abused.
I am not the cause of another's violent behavior.
I do not like it or want it.
I am an important human being.
I am a worthwhile woman.
I deserve to be treated with respect.
I do have power over my own life.
I can use my power to take good care of myself.
I can decide for myself what is best for me.
I can make changes in my life if I want to.
I am not alone. I can ask others to help me.
I am worth working for and changing for.
I deserve to make my own life safe and happy.
(New York: Anchor Press, 1979)

3. Creating Rituals of Healing and Cleansing

When creating a ritual it is helpful to consider the following:

171

a. What natural symbols are connected with this experience for me, e.g., darkness, fragmentation, the meaning of times and places?
b. What religious symbols or biblical passages might help bring meaning to the event?
c. What symbolic action would best convey this meaning?

4. *Praying the Psalms*

The following Psalms are helpful in individual and group prayer around issues of violence. Many women use only selected passages from them, omitting portions that seem to continue the cycle of violence: Psalms 22, 27, 55, 118, 140.

[1]From Ntozake Shange, *Nappy Edges* (New York: St. Martin's Press, 1977), p. 114.

[2]For a discussion of these issues, see Mary Pellauer, "Violence Against Women: The Theological Dimension," in *Christianity and Crisis* 439 (May 30, 1983), 206–212; and "A Theological Perspective on Sexual Assault," *Christianity and Crisis* 44 (June 25, 1984), 250–255. Also helpful are *Sexual Assault and Abuse: A Handbook for Clergy and Religious Professionals*, ed. Mary D. Pellauer, Barbara Chester, and Jane Boyajian (New York: Harper & Row, 1987); Rita-Lou Clarke, *Pastoral Care of Battered Women* (Philadelphia: Westminster Press, 1986); Lois Gehr Livezey, "Sexual and Family Violence: A Growing Issue for the Churches," *The Christian Century* (October 28, 1987), 938–942.

[3]Anonymous, "Crisis in Community: Responses to Rape," *Review for Religious* (November-December 1986), 870–871.

[4](New York: Simon and Schuster, 1983), p. 2.

[5]*Sexual Violence. The Unmentionable Sin* (New York: The Pilgrim Press, 1983), p. 209.

[6]Mary Pellauer, "A Theological Perspective on Sexual Assault," p. 253.

[7]Hummy, "A Totally White World," in *I Never Told Anyone. Writings By Women Survivors of Child Sexual Abuse*, ed. Ellen Bass and Louise Thornton (New York: Harper & Row, 1983), pp. 241–250.

[8]*Sojourners* 13 (November 1984), 24.

[9]A practical approach to the abused woman's religious questions is Marie M. Fortune, *Keeping the Faith. Questions and Answers for the Abused Woman* (San Francisco: Harper & Row, 1987).

[10]*In Memory of Her*, pp. 243ff. See also Susan Brooks Thistlethwaite, "Every Two Minutes: Battered Women and Feminist Interpretation," in *Feminist Interpretation of the Bible*, pp. 96–107.

[11]See *God and the Rhetoric of Sexuality* (Philadelphia: Fortress Press, 1978).

[12]P. 222.

[13]Two books which treat this topic are *Reweaving the Web of Life. Feminism and Nonviolence*, ed. Pam McAllister (Philadelphia: New Society Publishers, 1982), and *My Country Is The Whole World*. A videotape on "Nonviolent Response to Personal Assault" is also available from Pax Christi USA.

[14]*Reweaving the Web of Life*, p. 12.

9

The Problem of Anger

Anger is a difficult and troublesome emotion for most people, men as well as women. "Anger is a flood," the book of Proverbs tells us (27:4), and the church lists it as one of the seven deadly sins. The bible warns us not to be angry, and, if we are, not to let the sun go down on our anger. Yet in spite of admonitions, we continue to experience anger, and sunset frequently arrives before we have found a way to put it to rest.

While anger is a challenge for all Christians, it is especially problematic for women.[1] We have been discouraged from awareness of our anger and the direct expression of it. This suppression of anger results, in part, from the high value women place on caring and relationships. Anger is seen as endangering and perhaps destroying those relationships. What if we tell a spouse, a friend, a pastor, or a supervisor that we are angry? Will they be able to handle it, or will we lose their friendship and approval? We sense that anger will lead to conflict, and as women we have been taught that conflict is something frightening and evil. This reluctance to face conflict may prevent us from acknowledging and working through our anger.

Not only does anger threaten our relationships, it clashes

with our ideas of goodness and holiness. The image of the ideal or good woman extols patience, kindness, and caring; anger is out of place in such an image. People speak disparagingly of "angry women." Anger in women threatens others, and so is labeled unfeminine, immature, even hysterical. These taboos against women's direct expression of anger make it easier to turn the anger inward rather than risk disapproval and the loss of important relationships.

The inhibition of women's anger would not be so problematic if we grew up in a church and culture with few or isolated instances giving rise to anger. However, this is not the case. In addition to the situations that lead to anger in every person's life—frustrations at work, difficulties in relationships, obstacles that block our goals—women must deal with the reality of sexism. Each specific aspect of oppression—the slighting of our gifts for ministry because we are women, the official statements that reiterate women's secondary place in the church, the fear of physical abuse, the lack of opportunity for job advancement—can fuel the fires of anger. In *Anger. The Misunderstood Emotion*, Carol Tavris quotes one woman as saying:

> Everything, from the verbal assault on the street, to a 'well-meant' sexist joke your husband tells, to the lower pay you get at work (for doing the same job a man would be paid more for), to television commercials, to rock-song lyrics . . . everything seems to barrage your aching brain, which has fewer and fewer protective defenses to screen such things out.[2]

Since this increased awareness of situations generating anger is accompanied by prohibitions against expressing that anger directly, women fear anger. Sometimes we are not even aware that we are angry.

All these factors make anger a central concern in the spirituality of women. The issue of anger is tied to a woman's struggle to love others well without losing her own integrity, to her view of herself as a good or evil person, to her efforts to achieve personal peace and honesty in prayer, and to her struggle for justice and the coming of the reign of God. The way anger is dealt with in the spiritual direction context is also a touchstone for how well spiritual guides understand women's situation today. If a woman's anger is pacified, explained away, or seen simply as her personal problem in isolation from its cultural causes, the old destructive patterns of dealing with anger will continue.

Depending on a woman's personal experience with anger, the following can be helpful dimensions of spiritual guidance: (1) recognizing and validating anger, (2) exploring the personal and social origins of anger, (3) finding ways to use anger for spiritual growth, and (4) clarifying the relationship between anger and forgiveness. The goal of spiritual friendship is to help women accept the experience of anger and direct its energy toward healthy growth, good relationships, and creativity. As Travis says, we want to learn how to use the anger of hope to avoid falling into the anger of despair.

RECOGNIZING AND VALIDATING ANGER

As we have seen, a primary factor accounting for our difficulty in acknowledging and accepting anger is the fact that it seems incompatible with holiness. During a spiritual direction session a sister in her early fifties was describing problems she was experiencing in her prayer. She usually prayed early in the morning, from the scripture texts of the day. During the preceding few weeks, however, she had frequently become restless and unable to concentrate during prayer. Silence was uncomfortable, and she found herself stopping to get a cup of coffee, or terminating the attempt to pray altogether. This was uncharacteristic behavior for her, and she wondered if she was losing her ability to pray. When I asked her what else had been going on in her life during these weeks, it became apparent that she was angry, but not fully aware of this anger. Her administrator had changed her responsibilities without consulting her, moving her from the wing of the hospital where she was working effectively to another unit. She resented this action, but had said nothing about it. She felt she could not risk

177

the possible consequences of dealing directly with the situation, yet the injustice of it continued to bother her. Anger did not fit her ideal of a good religious. She felt guilty even acknowledging its existence.

This sister is not alone in the difficulty she experiences with reconciling anger and holiness. As one woman expressed it,

> When I was growing up I learned that if you loved someone you didn't get angry with them; and if you got angry, that meant you didn't love them.

Another woman found her inner peace disrupted by a relationship with a man who called her only when it was convenient for him and who made promises he never kept. At one point in recounting the way she accommodated him, she cried out, "Why am I so nice!" In exploring this issue she became aware of her spiritual ideal, "the good-girl self," as she called it. This ideal was reinforced in her early education and related to an image she had of Mary of Nazareth. However, another self was emerging, one that was willing to acknowledge the anger she felt when she was treated unfairly.

The psychological theories of Karen Horney help to illumine this ideal self as it functions in many women's spiritual lives. Horney believes that the desire to avoid conflict and disapproval causes certain emotions to be blocked, labeled wrong, and eventually repressed. This results in the creation of rigid self-ideals; the repressed need or emotion is expressed in characteristics that are the direct opposite of the hidden feeling. For example, repressed hostility is transformed into the self-ideal of being and acting totally loving and dutiful toward others. The most difficult aspect of change may be giving up exaggerated and unrealistic self-ideals. We may be busy trying to be perfect and blaming ourselves for not achieving that goal.[3]

This mixture of emotions helps explain why some women find it physically exhausting to be angry, and why it interferes with their ability to sleep, concentrate, or function well. We may fear that if we recognize our anger, after not acknowledging it for a long time, there will be an explosion. We also recognize on some level that anger signals the need for change in our actions and relationships, and such change may feel threatening. These conflicting feelings make anger an unpleasant experience; we would avoid it if we could. But when we do not acknowledge and express anger directly, it can take indirect forms and appear as depression, fatigue, or apathy.

An important function of spiritual direction is providing a safe place for a woman to explore and affirm her anger while she learns to use its energy in creative ways. This is especially important for those women who fear their anger will overwhelm them and others, or emerge in inappropriate and detructive ways. In the past, it was thought that venting anger was a helpful way to get rid of it. This theory is currently being challenged; venting may simply increase the anger, since it tells our body to keep it coming. Dealing with anger is not a matter of getting it out so that we can get rid of it; it is a matter of turning it from indirect and destructive forms of expression to those that are direct and constructive. While it is helpful to release the adrenalin created by the anger, this can be done in any number of physical activities—swimming, dancing, jogging, doing relaxation exercises, breathing deeply, cleaning the house, chopping wood. Since anger is a matter of both mind and body, we can continue to fuel the anger by mentally rehearsing the situation in which it occurred. This can often be exhausting and nonproductive. Instead of moving us forward, it keeps us stuck in a recycling of the pain.

What is a healthy Christian approach to anger? Anger is a message, a revelation. Looking at and understanding the conflict we experience is a key step in illuminating the situation we find ourselves in. What might God be revealing to me in this situation? How is my personhood being violated here? Or what valid needs of mine are not being met? If we are attempting to hear God's word, we must listen to anger as carefully as we listen to joy, peace, fear, and fatigue. This approach to anger has been articulated well by Fran Ferder. She speaks of anger as a gift.

As such it was purposefully and lovingly created and shaped by God as a source of energy, as a source of fire.

The only aspect of anger about which we have choices is how we let it move us. We do not have choices about whether or not we will experience it, unless we choose to cut off a very significant dimension of God's life in us.[4]

For many women, viewing anger as a gift of God rather than as an abnormal and sinful emotion requires a dramatic shift. We need new models to support such a change in perception. Ferder refers us to a central story from Jesus' life: Jesus' cleansing of the temple in John's gospel. In this story Jesus is clearly angry and does not hesitate to make the strength of his emotion known. It is an expression of his zeal for the reign of God. Our anger can contribute to the same purpose. First, however, we must acknowledge that we are angry. It is also helpful to know why.

EXPLORING THE ORIGINS OF OUR ANGER

Although we may initially experience anger as interfering with clear thinking, understanding the reasons for our anger can in fact lead to greater clarity about ourselves and our relationships. Spiritual direction can help women appreciate the personal and political origins of anger. Two key questions which help unlock these insights are: What am I really feeling? and Why am I feeling this way?

Recent research on anger illumines the first question, What am I really feeling? It indicates that anger is not a simple emotion. Many different feelings lie beneath the secondary response we name when we say, "I am angry." These emotions are fear, hurt, frustration, outrage, powerlessness. We may be feeling ignored, discounted, or treated unfairly. It is more helpful to identify these primary emotions and express our anger in terms of them. Anger is the instinct of self-preservation. It signals us that we are in danger, that our needs are not being met, that our rights are being violated, that we are allowing others to define us, or that unfair demands are being made upon us.

An example may help. Sue was a young woman who had belonged for several years to a fundamentalist Christian group, and was trying to live out the biblical ideal of love. During spiritual direction she described how she was feeling increasingly guilty about the way she related to a woman who rented a room in her house. For several weeks they had grown more and more silent with one another, and Sue found that she avoided her housemate and barely greeted her when she came home. It took some time for Sue to realize that she was angry but afraid to admit it since she saw it as a sign that she was failing in love. When she was able to recognize and accept her anger, it helped her to look more closely at the underlying feelings. Beneath her anger Sue found that she felt hurt by the fact that her housemate ignored her and never shared anything that was happening in her life. Sue also felt that she was being treated unfairly because her housemate was not abiding by the rental agreement, which she acknowledged had not been very clear in the first place. Sorting out her underlying emotions helped Sue clarify the sources of her anger and pointed to some actions she might take in expressing it positively.

These insights can help us clarify the personal roots of our anger. But anger is not simply a personal problem. As with other issues in our lives, women need to recognize the political origins of much anger. A woman was once referred to me by a professor in a program in which she was enrolled. She told me that he wanted me to do some healing work with her around her anger against the church, which came out frequently in her class comments. He had suggested to the woman that she must have had some negative childhood experiences that were in need of healing. His approach implied that the anger was the woman's personal problem and that the solution lay in uncovering the psychic causes.

While many of us do indeed carry with us baggage from the past, we cannot understand our anger if we look only within ourselves for its origins. Such an approach runs the risk of muting the moral power of anger as a force against injustice. While it might have intersected with earlier hurts and rejections in her life, this woman's anger had a sufficient cause in the insults and barriers she was indeed experiencing in the in-

181

stitutional church. It needed to be affirmed as legitimate and as founded on the reality of injustice. For many women such acknowledgement is an important part of eliminating the guilt they feel about being angry. Once this point is established, it is possible to evaluate the effectiveness of various ways of expressing anger.

Recent reflection on assertiveness programs for women illumines this question of the personal and political roots of anger.[5] The direct expression of anger is a particular instance of the more general area of assertive behavior. Such direct expression of emotions is a choice in favor of clear communication. It is a goal of assertiveness training for women since that training is aimed at helping them express their feelings honestly and comfortably. During the past two decades, assertiveness training has been one of the most popular feminist therapy programs and the subject of numerous self-help books. Countless women have participated in assertiveness training workshops in the United States and Europe. Most of these programs are based on the assumption that women lack assertiveness and do not know how to stand up for their own rights. However, recent research challenges the view that males are assertive and females are nonassertive. Rather, the research shows that women have certain assets when it comes to assertion, and that they are nonassertive only under certain conditions: Women have greater difficulty than men in refusing requests, expressing negative feelings, and setting limits. On the other hand, women assert themselves more easily than men in giving expressions of love, affection, and approval to others.

More directly related to our point about the relationship between the personal and the political is the growing realization that focusing on areas of nonassertive behavior in women is not enough. Such an approach is based on the assumption that if individual women change, society's attitudes toward them will change. In fact, there is now a growing body of research that suggests a strong bias against assertive women. The results of their assertive behavior may therefore not be positive, not because of a woman's deficits, but because of society's deficits. This reinforces the conviction that we have to go beyond the personal and work for societal change.

When half the population is targeted as needing to change their behavior in order to gain fair treatment by the system, we have to ask what system are those individuals trying to fit.[6]

Critics of assertiveness training suggest that individual work is not enough because it focuses on symptoms and blames the victim rather than addressing the larger issues and treating the system. This must be kept in mind as we look at ways in which women can direct the energy of their anger in positive ways.

USING ANGER FOR SPIRITUAL GROWTH

Like other aspects of reality, the experience and expression of anger has been distorted by the dichotomies imposed on human existence. Adrienne Rich, in her poem "Integrity," describes the hope of breaking through such dichotomies

Anger and tenderness: my selves.
And now I can believe they breathe in me
as angels, not polarities.
Anger and tenderness: the spider's genius
to spin and weave in the same action
from her own body, anywhere—
even from a broken web.[7]

Stereotypes about female and male behavior have restricted this aspect of human life along with others. When we search for creative ways to deal with anger, we find few models.

As women acquire the freedom to look at anger in fresh ways, they are developing new approaches to it. One woman describes her imaginative method.

The male hierarchy just angers me. My feminine spirit is stifled and cries constantly. I have gotten to the point of naming the different people inside of me—priestess, prophet, feminist, mother. Then I speak to them and say, 'Seth, it is not your season yet;

183

I am going to let Elizabeth speak to these men right now.' It works for me and I am very creative with my energies. Each staff I have worked with finds that I do express what I feel, but I also am speaking the truth. I time things well.

What this woman's comments convey is the creative effort to preserve both the legitimacy of anger and the importance of relationships.

Through the spiritual direction process we can learn not only to look at our anger and accept it without guilt or self-recrimination, but to use it creatively for our own spiritual growth and our work for the reign of God. Miriam Greenspan describes this use of anger. Like love, anger takes many shapes, she says. There are hidden and self-destructive forms such as depression.

> But there is another form of anger, the other side of which is love. Not only a growing love for ourselves and each other as women, but also a growing realization that we are all of us—men and women alike—mutually interdependent. This is not a rigid closing off of our energies but an opening up to a respectful compassion for ourselves as women, and a loving struggle with the men in our lives. Anger is the fuel we need to burn in the struggle to create a society without victims.[8]

We may have little choice about whether we will feel angry or not, since anger arises spontaneously and physically. However, once we are aware of this emotion, we have a choice about what we will do.

Anger is a state of being highly energized, and we can act in a number of ways when we are in that state. As Tavris summarizes it:

> The moral use of anger, I believe, requires an awareness of choice and an embrace of reason. It is knowing when to become angry—'this is wrong, this I will pro-

test'—and when to make peace; when to take action, and when to keep silent; knowing the likely cause of one's anger and not berating the blameless.[9]

This choice also involves discriminating between the sources of anger we can do something about, and those we cannot. Aware of the limits of our energy, we learn to recognize when an expression of anger can be effective and when it is a waste of time.

The creative use of anger also includes the sense that we are addressing the source of the grievance. No matter what we do with our anger in the short run, it will not have served its purpose unless we address the situations and relationships which gave rise to the anger in the first place. The native American poet, Joy Harjo, writes of the sufferings of poor families where women face not only the struggle to provide bread and a roof, but where violence and alcohol make domestic life hell.

> angry women are building
> houses of stones
> they are grinding the mortar
> between straw-thin teeth
> and broken families[10]

Out of their anger women are strengthening their determination to change destructive patterns.

Anger that comes from a clear sense of injustice requires the channeling of its energy into alleviating that injustice. However, we may feel powerless to do anything about the situations that anger us. In her helpful book, *The Dance of Anger*, Harriet Lerner provides some approaches to assist women in dealing creatively with their anger.[11] Lerner emphasizes that anger operates within a system of relationships. Our behavior helps to support the behavior of others. This is what she calls the dance of anger. While we usually cannot change the behavior of others, Lerner says, we can change our own behavior and thus make it impossible for the dance to continue as before.

> We cannot make another person change his or her
> steps to an old dance, but if we change our steps, the
> dance no longer can continue in the same predictable
> pattern.[12]

This approach focuses on changing patterns of relationship
rather than on blaming ourselves or the other persons involved. For example, a friend of mine who is the mother of
three young children was exhausted and resentful because of
their constant demands. As a way of dealing with her resentment and anger, she decided to change the way she related to
them. She began to set limits and then she stuck with them.
A woman who constantly picked up the pieces so that her
male supervisor looked good, meanwhile resenting the fact
that it was her talent and ingenuity he received credit for, simply stopped rescuing him.

Women have begun to change their behavior in relation to
the church as well—making their discontent with sexism public, refusing to allow their experiences to be trivialized, contributing to biblical research and theology which illumine
women's role in the church, targeting their donations to wom-
en's projects. As women change their steps in the old dance, it
becomes more difficult for the patterns to continue.

But as Lerner points out, systems usually have an invest-
ment in our staying exactly the same. We can expect therefore
that they will intensify their resistance as we change our behavior. Since they want the dance to go on as before, they will
dance the same steps more insistently as we change our own
part in it. This is a way of saying: "You're wrong; change back
or else . . . " Lerner describes this powerful emotional coun-
terforce as predictable and universal. If women are not prepared for it, however, such resistance can surprise and defeat
them.

Women need to recognize that expressing anger frequently carries a practical price. We receive rewards for what
is considered appropriate behavior; if we show anger we risk
losing real rewards. Women who are already in poverty or situations of physical abuse are being realistic when they recognize the dangers involved in expressing their anger directly. As

Jean Baker Miller insists, it is not useful to urge people who are in subordinate positions to conduct conflict as if they were not powerless and dependent. It is very difficult to initiate conflict when you are totally dependent on an individual or group for your elemental material and psychological means of existence.[13]

Viewing anger within patterns of relationship helps us understand another aspect of it. How we feel after expressing our anger depends a great deal on how it is received. Many people are as uncomfortable with another person's anger as they are with their own. They do not know how to respond. We may work with a woman in spiritual direction around her own expressions of anger and she may learn to handle them very well. Yet her interactions with a colleague, a husband, a friend, or a parent may leave her feeling inadequate and depressed because of the way her anger is received by them. Sometimes direct expressions merely worsen both the situation and our own feelings; another approach is then necessary. Lerner lists some questions that are helpful in sorting out approaches to anger:

> What am I really angry about?
> What is the problem and whose problem is it?
> How can I express my anger in a way that will not leave me feeling helpless and powerless?
> When I'm angry, how can I clearly communicate my position without becoming defensive or attacking?
> What risks and losses might I face if I become clearer and more assertive?
> If getting angry is not working for me, what can I do differently?[14]

These questions are useful as well for discernment in spiritual direction. They spell out the Christian ideal of telling the truth with love (Eph 4:15–16).

One aspect of discernment in relation to anger is how closely a woman will be associated with the institutional church. The continuum of involvement with the church runs all the way from simply belonging to working in a ministry that takes a woman close to the center of church structures.[15]

For example, a woman who had worked in a diocesan chancery office for several years found that because of her anger with the church she needed to leave that job, but that she could still manage to be active in her parish as a volunteer. Other women can only attend liturgies on an intermittent basis or must stay away from such celebrations completely for a time. Still other women choose to change denominations or to leave the church completely. We often turn to spiritual friends for help in making these choices.

Women sometimes feel anger toward a person, perhaps a parent, who is no longer living. They cannot express their anger directly, yet they feel that something in the relationship is unfinished. In these cases, writing a letter that is later destroyed, speaking to the person in an empty chair, or developing some other ritual is a move toward closure.

All of these approaches can help us channel the energy of anger into spiritual growth and creative action.

ANGER AND FORGIVENESS

Like self-sacrifice, forgiveness is a Christian ideal that has been defined in ways restrictive for women; in the process the meaning of forgiveness has been distorted and, in fact, trivialized. Women have at times been led to believe that forgiveness is a one-time action that can follow quickly on the heels of being wronged. In spiritual direction, they frequently struggle with this, saying: "I know I should forgive this person, but I can't," or "I've tried to forgive, but the pain won't go away, and the anger keeps coming back when I think about it."

Forgiveness can in fact be a lengthy process with a number of stages.[16] One woman describes the shape this process takes for her.

> I take time for journaling, healing and prayer. I state my needs while working toward mutual reconciliation and joy. I don't accept what is destructive and devaluing of my person.

Forgiveness rests on awareness of the hurt or pain we have experienced and any anger that accompanies it. It moves to a recognition of how this has affected the relationship and what actions we must take. Finally, a time of healing may be necessary.

The act of forgiving is a way of saying that we will no longer dwell on the pain inflicted on us, or use the experience of being wronged as a weapon in the relationship. In other words, we will not harm another in return for being harmed. Forgiveness does not require that we excuse or minimize the wrong done to us, or take more than our share of responsibility for what happens in relationships. Nor does it imply that we will necessarily continue to relate to a person or stay in a harmful relationship. Because of the importance we give to affiliation, women experience the loss of a relationship as the loss of a dimension of the self. Some relationships must end, however, for the good of all involved, and recognition of this fact is a dimension of forgiveness.

Forgiveness usually requires a healing process, though it may vary in length. Ritual has been an important part of that healing for many women with whom I have worked in spiritual direction. One woman wanted to be free of some bitterness that she had experienced for years in a relationship. As she thought about this process of letting go, she recalled how as a child she used to take her hurts and pains and attach them to small wooden boats that she set out to sea. It helped her to revive this childhood ritual, this time attaching statements about her more recent feelings of resentment to the boats she made.

Once when I was working with a group of women on the use of ritual, one woman told us that she had developed a healing ritual around the pain of her divorce. On her wedding anniversary she went to the church where she had been married, and walked through the ceremony again alone. This time she expressed her pain, let go of some of her idealistic notions regarding marriage, and asked for forgiveness where she was responsible for the difficulties that led to the divorce. Several women in the group were surprised that she had the courage to do this. Another woman was trying to move toward forgiveness in a relationship that had ended with no opportunity for her to express her emotions directly. As part of the healing process, she wrote out her feelings, burned the letter, and in the ashes planted flower seeds. It was a death/resurrection ritual that helped her deal with some of her feelings.

In commenting on the problems we all experience in dealing with anger, Jean Baker Miller offers an interesting challenge.[17] Neither women nor men, she says, have been able to experience or express the sort of anger that may be possible but which we are not yet able to conceptualize. The constraints for women are different and more restrictive than those for men, but men also learn to suppress and deflect anger. Our culture will not be able to solve its problems with anger, Miller believes, until we encourage each sex to examine and understand its own experience of anger more fully and truthfully. Meeting this challenge in new ways is a central part of working for the reign of God in our midst.

FOR PRAYER AND REFLECTION

1. Praying About Our Anger

Choose for the subject of your prayer a recent experience of anger. In the presence of God, reflect on this experience: What were you angry about? What feelings lay beneath the anger? What is God revealing to you in this anger? Acknowledge the feelings before God and let them be your own, a part of who you are.

Then decide on one thing you can change about your actions or responses in the situation that gave rise to the anger. In other words, how can you alter your steps in this dance of anger so that the dance cannot go on as before? As you weigh your choices, be aware of any areas of yourself that fear and resist change. Consider your choice before God, and then ask for strength to carry it out.

2. *Journaling About Anger*

Sometimes it is easier to write about our anger, since writing is a more controlled medium than speech. Journal about your anger. You may want to write your history of anger, including messages you heard about its religious meaning, ways you saw anger expressed or not expressed in your family, responses you have received from others when you have expressed anger, and your fears and hopes about the anger you experience in your life.

It may be helpful to draw a picture of your anger, and share this picture and your responses to it in a spiritual direction session.

3. *Expressing Anger in Movement*

Anger is a physical experience, a rush of energy and adrenalin meant to motivate, protect and empower for action. We have all learned how to clamp down physically and withhold our anger so as not to harm others. Eventually, we end up harming ourselves by bottling up this powerful force and not accessing it for choiceful living. This exercise suggests one way to express your anger in movement and, in doing so, to restore the flow of energy throughout your body. You then have a choice for how to direct this flow into creative action in your life.

For this exercise, choose a safe environment where noise will not disturb others. Begin by grounding, feeling your legs connected to the earth (see the exercise in Chapter 2). Notice where in your body you feel tight, held, restricted. These are the places from which you will focus on bringing out expression.

Now take a pillow. Hold the pillow over your head and arch back slightly, knees bent to maintain grounding. As if shooting an arrow, propel your top half forward with force, striking the floor (or bed) with the pillow. Let out a growl or aggressive sound. Repeat this as many times as you have energy for. Each time focus on bringing out expression from a different body part—jaw, shoulders and arms, belly, pelvis, legs.

The more comfortable you become, experiment with other ways to move and express anger, e.g., stomping or kicking, biting, etc. When you are complete, practice grounding and softening again. Notice how your body feels now, and write results in your journal.

When working in a group, stand in a fairly large circle and use the energy of the group to support you. You can even take turns leading different aggressive movements that you discover. Share verbally with others as you complete.

(This exercise was created by Betsey Beckman; see pp. 48–49 and 109–110.)

4. Jesus' Anger: A Gospel Meditation

Meditate on the story of Jesus cleansing the temple in John 2:13–16. The following questions may help you enter into the story: What does the temple symbolize to you? In what areas of your life can you identify with Jesus' anger? How do you feel zeal for God's house? How are you called to express this zeal? What are your convictions about violence and nonviolence in relation to the expression of this zeal?

NOTES

[1]See Alexandra G. Kaplan, et al., "Women and Anger in Psychotherapy," in *Women Changing Therapy*, pp. 29–40.

[2](New York: Simon & Schuster, 1982), p. 246.

[3]*See Our Inner Conflicts* (New York: W.W. Norton, 1945); *Neurosis and Human Growth* (New York: W.W. Norton, 1950).

[4]"Zeal for Your House Consumes Me: Dealing with Anger as a Woman in the Church," in *Women in the Church I*, ed. Madonna Kolbenschlag (Washington, DC: The Pastoral Press, 1987), p. 97.

[5]Iris Goldstein Fodor, "Assertiveness Training for the Eighties: Moving Beyond the Personal," in *Handbook of Feminist Therapy. Women's Issues in Psychotherapy*, ed. Lynne Bravo Rosewater and Lenore E. A. Walker (New York: Springer Publishing Co., 1985), pp. 257–265.

[6]"Assertiveness Training," p. 261.

[7]Adrienne Rich, *The Fact of a Doorframe. Poems Selected and New. 1950–1984* (New York: W.W. Norton & Company, 1984), p. 274.

[8]*A New Approach to Women and Therapy*, p. 315.

[9]*Anger. The Misunderstood Emotion*, p. 253.

[10]"Conversations Between Here and Home," in *Voices of Women. Poetry By and About Third World Women*, p. 25.

[11](New York: Harper & Row, 1985).

[12]*The Dance of Anger*, p. 13.

[13]*Toward A New Psychology of Women*, p. 122.

[14]*The Dance of Anger*, p. 4.

[15]A description of different levels of engagement can be found in Carolyn Osiek, R.S.C.J., *Beyond Anger. On Being a Feminist in the Church* (New York: Paulist Press, 1986), pp. 25–43.

[16]Helpful insights on anger and forgiveness are presented in Evelyn Eaton Whitehead and James D. Whitehead, *Seasons*

of Strength. New Visions of Adult Christian Maturing (New York: Doubleday, 1984), pp. 115–128.

[17]"The Construction of Anger in Women and Men," *Work in Progress* (Wellesley, MA: Stone Center for Developmental Services and Studies, 1983), p. 8.

10

Grandmothers, Mothers, and Daughters:
The Spiritual Legacy

Peggy was talking in spiritual direction about her desire to become more directly involved in justice issues. At one point she asked herself, "Where is this call coming from?" "Why do I feel so strongly that I must do something besides donate money to worthwhile causes?" As she explored these questions, Peggy made an important discovery regarding the origins of her spirituality. Her desire to help those in need was not rooted primarily in scripture, theology, or church teachings, although all of these had influenced her. The call came most urgently from memories of her own grandmother. She could recall vividly how her grandmother had welcomed anyone in need to a meal in her home, how she had visited sick and aging neighbors, and how she had seen that extra apples and potatoes on the farm were given to the poor. Peggy realized that her relationship with her grandmother had instilled certain values in her, and she wanted to keep this legacy alive in some way.

Like Peggy, Barbara also discovered some important dimensions of her spiritual inheritance. News that her mother had a terminal illness led to a painful reassessment of their relationship. Up to that time, Barbara had felt mainly resentment toward her mother. She hated the way her mother put herself down and then manipulated others to get what she wanted. But in her grief at the thought of losing her, Barbara began to see that there was another side to her mother; she began to reflect as well on the positive things her mother had given her. She had inherited her mother's capacity for creative gift-giving, her freedom to believe yet question the ways of God, and her courage in the face of hardships. Before her mother's death Barbara was able to give thanks for the continuity, while at the same time recognizing the differences in their spiritual paths.

We are linked not only physically, but spiritually as well, to our mothers, our grandmothers, and all the women who have come before us. With them we share a common gender identity and the social roles and expectations that go with it. Mothers and grandmothers provide some of our most compelling models of what it means to be a woman, as well as the spiritual opportunities and restrictions of that womanhood. But most histories, including biblical genealogies, are stories of the male line, not the female; the legacy of women appears primarily as a legacy of weakness. One of our challenges is to transform it into a legacy of strength. What do we know of the faith lives of our mothers, our grandmothers, our great-grandmothers? We hear many stories of fathers and sons, even in the bible. The stories of mothers and daughters are only beginning to be told.[1]

An important aspect of spiritual friendship is the discovery of this legacy, the integration into our lives of its positive aspects, and the healing of its painful dimensions. We will look at three ways of working with these issues in spiritual direction: (1) reclaiming the spiritual heritage we received from our grandmothers, mothers, or the mother figures in our lives, (2) healing the painful aspects of this legacy, and (3) integrating insights from motherhood into our common spiritual tradition.

RECLAIMING OUR HERITAGE

In counseling circles today increasing attention is being given to work with our family of origin, the family in which we were born and raised.[2] The influence of that family extends well beyond our childhood. Even after we leave our family and begin an independent life, we carry with us its formative influence as a permanent endowment. Not only is it part of our genetic makeup, it is the deepest part of our cultural and religious formation as well. It shapes the way we view ourselves, others, and the world. Usually there is ongoing contact with members of our family of origin which keeps the relationships and their ramifications alive, and even after the death of a parent we continue to struggle with many aspects of this relationship.

In spiritual direction, as well as in counseling, women will very likely be dealing at one time or another with all of the relationships in their family, those with grandfathers, fathers, and brothers as well as those with grandmothers, mothers, and sisters. However, here we will be looking primarily at the women in the family of origin because of their special significance for women and because relationships between women have so often been trivialized or ignored.

When I asked two different women recently to tell me about their most important religious experiences, each replied by recalling stories of her grandmother. The first woman summarized her experience briefly.

> A very early and continuing ritual in my family was for one of us girls to go to my grandmother's room after dinner. While we brushed her hair, she prayed in Chinook to God as Mother, in French from her bible, and in English her litany of petitions. This was key for me in relating to God as Mother throughout my life.

The second woman told her experience more at length.

> My grandmother was a very important influence on my spiritual life. When I was little we lived in the

197

same apartment building. My grandparents lived on the floor below and went to 6 a.m. Mass. My mother was not a morning person, so I would take my two younger sisters downstairs for our first breakfast with our grandparents on their return from Mass. We would have tea and toast with marmalade, read the obituaries and make plans for wakes and funerals that week. My grandmother specialized in this spiritual work of mercy.

Various transitions followed until I was nine years old. My grandparents moved next door to us in north Seattle. By this time Grandma was in her 80's and in poor health. I would go to her house in the evening to pray the rosary and various devotions to saints in flickering candlelight with lots of statues, especially St. Theresa the Little Flower. Grandma was unfailingly patient and generous. She'd let me fix her hair and dress her up in various night gowns and bed jackets. I would help my mother bathe her.

She kept round white mints in the top drawer of her dresser and I could have them. If you admired anything of hers she gave it to you. This drove her children nuts, as the Christmas presents they bought her were often gone by March. Grandma kept a stash of money around to send to the poor.

In August, 1959, when I was twelve years old, Grandma had her final stroke. She could not talk, move, or open her eyes. The family decided to keep her at home to die in her own bed. We sat with her and held her hand, talking and praying. On a brilliant, sunny morning, August 28, my grandfather called to say she had just died. We raced across the wet grass to her house, her room. She looked so beautiful . . . so happy. I felt her spirit still there. It was as if heaven and earth were met in that room. This experience has been a watershed in my thinking about death.

Experiences with their grandmothers shaped, in very significant ways, these women's attitudes toward God and death.

Our spirituality is influenced not only by our grandmothers, but often more profoundly by our mothers, or those women who functioned as mother figures in our lives. When asked about the women who have played a key role in their faith journeys many women talk about their mothers. This is true even when they have a hard time relating to their mothers, or find that their own spiritual paths have moved in very different directions. Many women no longer practice the devotions they learned from their mothers or share the same doctrinal convictions, but they still refer to their mother's spiritual influence as a foundation, the ground work for all that followed. Women speak of being strongly affected by their mothers' deep faith, trust, and self-giving. One woman phrased it this way.

> I think my mother was the most important influence in shaping my spirituality. She is a model of Christian love—agape love—always thinking of others before herself and also encouraging all of us to be the best person we can—what God meant us to be.

Another woman speaks of her mother in a similar way.

> She taught me about God and Mary from the earliest years of my life. Her love of God was a lived daily love. She was a professional singer and entertainer and did not always go to church, but she raised us in the Catholic faith. The church is my heritage.

Both women found that they understood their own faith stories better when they saw their connection with their mothers' lives.

Issues surrounding the women in our families arise in a variety of ways in spiritual direction. Sometimes we must deal with the anger we feel toward our mothers. Sometimes we are searching for a way to relate to them with love and faithfulness in spite of the conflicts we experience. The death of a mother is frequently described by women as one of their most moving religious experiences. Mother-figures also appear in women's dreams. All of these occasions provide opportunities for understanding and appropriating our spiritual legacy more fully. This can be done in a number of different ways, but women have found the following especially helpful: (1) recalling and journaling about their earliest memories of grandmothers, mothers, and aunts, and the influence these had on their own beliefs; (2) learning more about how their grandmother's or mother's own faith was shaped and expressed, for example, by asking their mothers about their childhood—where they went to church, what it meant to them, what values they were taught; (3) becoming aware of what they have rejected and what they have retained from the religious legacy of the women in their family.

Two recent autobiographies by contemporary American women give central importance to the life stories of their mothers: Maxine Hong Kingston's *The Woman Warrior: Memoirs of a Girlhood Among Ghosts* and Kim Chernin's *In My Mother's House: A Daughter's Story.* Both mothers are immigrants. After emigrating from China, Kingston's mother, Brave Orchid, had six children after the age of forty-five and worked long hours in a laundry. Chernin's mother, Rose, was born in a Jewish ghetto in Russia, and after coming to America was imprisoned during the McCarthy era. As Jeanne Barker-Nunn shows, their daughters are entrusted with their mothers' stories, a legacy they find both empowering and burdensome.

> Kingston sets out to write her own story and finds herself telling her mother's; Chernin begins writing her mother's story and ends telling her own. They discover that they need to tell the one to tell the other; individual lives appear to have little meaning out of the context of history and family. Nor does the contextual or embedded feel of these works end there. What appears as an almost primal struggle between mother and daughter takes place against a backdrop of many generations of women.[3]

Although Kingston and Chernin must break with many of their mothers' views of the world, they also convey a moving sense of the continuities they share. It is through and against their mothers' stories that they come to understand themselves.

This legacy is ancient and complex, but a woman's faith story is incomplete without it. Our spirituality is enriched when we notice the strengths of women all around us, especially our mothers, grandmothers, sisters, and daughters. They are beacons on our journey of liberation.

HEALING THE PAINFUL LEGACY

When women talk about their mothers in spiritual direction, they do not usually begin with an awareness of their contributions to their spiritual lives. Rather, they are often angry with their mothers or hurt by something they have said or done; in light of this they are finding it hard to love and relate to them. Their mothers have not met their needs. They have placed unrealistic demands on them, interfered with their lives, or embodied negative qualities daughters fear they will imitate.

In their study of *Women and Self-Esteem*, Linda Sanford and Mary Ellen Donovan report that when they asked women they interviewed who their primary role model was, many told them, "Anybody but my mother." They cite one study which shows that sixty-three percent of the women interviewed said they consciously avoided patterning themselves after their mothers. Yet Sanford and Donovan say that when they pursued the subject further, nearly everyone revealed that her mother's impact was probably the greatest of all. They repeatedly heard comments like, "My mother is probably the most important figure in my life," whether in a positive or a negative sense.[4]

In her studies of the mother/daughter relationship, Irene Stiver comes to some of the same conclusions. Women, she says, are frequently unforgiving of their mothers' offenses against them. Girls watch their mothers being denigrated in the family and realize that becoming an adult like their mother has no future reward or superior power.

> The daughter feels outrage and fury as a consequence and accuses her mother, 'Why didn't you fight harder?' That is indeed a frequent lament of my women patients. While reporting with some feeling the ways in which their fathers demeaned their mothers, they express anger at their mothers, saying, 'Why did she take it? Why didn't she leave him? It's her fault.'[5]

At the same time, Stiver says, strong bonds are established between mothers and daughters which continue throughout life. Mothers and daughters maintain close, if complex, ties.

In light of these realities, a woman's spiritual challenge is often that of letting go of images of perfect mothers and perfect daughters who fully meet each other's needs and expectations. This means learning to view our mothers with compassion. Such compassion grows with recognition that similar social forces have shaped both our mothers' and our own lives. We have lived in a patriarchal culture for as long as we and our mothers and grandmothers can remember. In such a context we sometimes see only our mothers' weaknesses, not their strengths. We miss the social oppression they had to face and instead blame them for everything wrong with them and us. Some forms of traditional counseling have merely reinforced this blaming tendency. Only recently have we begun to question our mothers' hardships or lack of power. It helps to see our mothers in their own cultural and religious context, to understand why they were devalued, and what images of women they internalized and passed on to us.

A mother's attitude toward her own body and sexuality is also crucial to the way a daughter thinks of herself in these areas. Women transfer to their female children their own feelings about what it means to be female. For many women this translates into a legacy of fear and mistrust of the body. The heritage of viewing the female cycles of menstruation, birth, and menopause as negative is passed on from mother to daughter. Women will often bring to spiritual direction issues related to these cycles. In *Becoming Woman: The Quest for Spiritual Wholeness in Female Experience,* Penelope Washbourn argues that for a woman the most significant life crises are associated with having a female body.[6] There are spiritual questions implicit within these crises; they challenge us to discern both the graceful and the negative dimensions of female sexuality.

Menstruation, for example, is a new body experience that is often accompanied by anxiety. Many women struggle with the emotional and physical changes that precede and accompany it. But menstruation can also be seen as bringing a new power that is sacred, one that calls for a symbolic, interpretive framework. In menstruation women experience their own bodily rhythms; they bleed without dying. Early cultures marked menstruation's onset with a rite of passage. Likewise, the spiritual challenges accompanying menopause relate to our society's negative view of aging women, a view based on the glorification of a youthful sexual image and woman's role as child-bearer. Finding wisdom in the later years means that a woman must move beyond such cultural sexism and affirm her gifts as a mature woman of faith.

One of the tasks of spiritual direction is to help women in the many seasons of their lives integrate their bodily experience with their spirituality. While expressing their anger at the way these issues were dealt with in their homes, women are finding ways to reverse and heal that tradition: recovering the sacred symbolism of blood and viewing menstruation as a blessing and not a curse, preparing rituals for their own daughters for the beginning of menstruation, attempting to separate out what a patriarchal culture has told them they are to experience during their bodily cycles from what their actual experiences are.

The mother/daughter relationship is part of the larger issue of being proud to be a woman and reclaiming our appreciation of women. As Dorothy Dinnerstein says in *The Mermaid and the Minotaur,*

What stops men from being our brothers also stops us from being each other's sisters. To ignore this fact—to identify the male as the sole source of our female sense of being hated and despised—is dangerously comforting; it encourages women to suppress important tensions among themselves which are then bound at some point to explode. For sisterhood to be truly powerful, the internal obstacles to human female solidarity must be faced, not evaded. What we ignore or deny at our peril is that women share men's anti-female feelings—usually in a mitigated form, but deeply nevertheless.[7]

Some women discover that the relationships with women in their family are part of a more general mistrust of female closeness; they find it difficult to love other women. This negative attitude toward women leads them to deny the sacred not only in themselves but also in other women. They do not want to see women preach or be ordained; they avoid receiving communion from a woman.

While teaching courses on Feminism and Christian Spirituality I have had several women tell me that their anger is not directed at men; rather, they find it hard to like women. One sister, who had been a member of a religious congregation for many years, said that the pain she needed to heal resulted from the way she had been treated by the women who had exercised authority in her community. Another woman said that while she found women's groups challenging and helpful, she also feared being in a group with other women. Her first response was to see herself in competition with them, and she was embarrassed to have to admit that she did not really think she liked women.

Healing the pain in mother/daughter relationships is foundational for learning to relate positively to all women.[8] On the social level such healing calls for a change in male/female relationships, especially in the family. It can also be approached on an individual level. If a mother is still living, it is frequently helpful simply to talk with her in depth about her life, gathering information about what she believed, how she viewed her life as a woman, what was going on in her life at critical times in our own relationship with her, and how she dealt with problems similar to our own. The goal is simply to understand, not to challenge or argue relative merits.

If a mother is no longer living, we may need to relate to her in a letter that is never sent, in a ritual, or in remembering. In her poem, "My Mother's Body," Marge Piercy tells of how, at her mother's death, she walked through the rooms of memory, and spoke to her mother:

> All I feared was being stuck in a box
> with a lid. A good woman appeared to me
> indistinguishable from a dead one
> except that she worked all the time.
>
> Your payday never came. Your dreams ran
> with bright colors like Mexican cottons
> that bled onto the drab sheets of the day
> and would not bleach with scrubbing.
>
> . . . .
>
> This body is your body, ashes now
> and roses, but alive in my eyes, my breasts,
> my throat, my thighs. You run in me
> a tang of salt in the creek waters of my blood,
>
> you sing in my mind like wine. What you
> did not dare in your life you dare in mine.[9]

Like Piercy, many daughters now live out in their own lives dreams that their mothers never dared even to dream. This is their way of continuing the legacy.

Ritual is another path to healing. One young woman discovered, as she began reading on feminism and spirituality, that she was angry at her mother because she never stood up for herself and always gave in to a domineering husband. As a daughter she was expected to follow the same pattern, for example, by doing household chores which were not expected of her brothers. The woman spent some weeks journaling about the experiences she remembered from her childhood which gave rise to this anger. Then she wanted to ritually celebrate her new insights and the beginning of some healing. She realized after she had developed the ritual that her family would not be ready to enact it with her, but it served as a hopeful vision of the kind of change in relationships she thought they might work toward. The ritual was this: The woman along with all the other women in her family, including her mother, were to be seated at the family table and served a meal by the men in her family. When the meal was finished the women would all remain seated while her father and brothers cleared the table and did the dishes. Then the men would return and join the women at the table.

All of these approaches—becoming aware of the conditions of our mothers' lives, talking with our mothers and grandmothers, taking time to remember, enacting rituals—can heal and strengthen women's legacy.

INTEGRATING INSIGHTS FROM MOTHERHOOD INTO SPIRITUALITY

A mother of several small children who was enrolled in a graduate theology course once told me that she often felt stupid and apologetic in class because she could not draw on an extensive background in theology and ministry the way the other students could. Being a mother seemed to be a liability, since no one ever mentioned children or what could be learned from raising and relating to them. Ironically, this was a course in which the emphasis was on experience as a starting point for theology.

Carol Ochs recounts a similar experience in *Women and Spirituality*.[10] When she studied the western spiritual tradition, she was appalled to find that no text was written from the viewpoint of a happily married mother. In light of that fact, she began to reflect on the question: How much of what I believe about reality—about the value of life and its meaning—is the result of having lived in marriage for nearly twenty-five years, and having raised two daughters to adulthood? Would the saints, she wonders, still have come up with the "purgative way" if they had raised a child to adulthood? She is convinced that women can draw on their experiences, such as mothering, to contribute to and correct traditional spirituality. The tradition presents a limited view of the spiritual life.

Many women share this conviction. One aspect of spiritual friendship is helping women who are mothers understand their own spirituality better and find ways to enrich our common spiritual heritage with the insights that come from being a mother or grandmother. When women themselves are asked about the spiritual impact of motherhood, they acknowledge concrete gifts. Among these are learning more of the dimensions of love, experiencing what it means both to hold, bond and nurture and to let go and take risks, and finding oneself involved in the miracle of creating life. Many women find the birth of each child to be a major religious experience. In addition, being a mother reveals their best and worst selves to them and allows them to know how they are like God as nurturing, strong, and loving, and how they are not.

Different mothers describe the influence of mothering on their spirituality in the following ways.

> My motherhood—or the reality of the responsibility of children has made me aware of *my* dependence and humanity. In parenthood I have been struck with being co-participator, co-creator with God in the celebration of life.

> I have a lot more sympathy for God! I am also inclined to think that growth is ongoing and mistakes are inevitable and that is OK. I am not afraid to yell at God when I'm feeling thwarted or frustrated, since my kids can yell at me without endangering *my* love for them.

> I think more in terms of the future and the need to act on this world to preserve it and improve it for my daughter, to ensure that she will have a world to live in.

> Children keep you humble. As a mother I sometimes see my narrowness and inflexibility in my interaction

with my children. Sometimes I'm at a complete loss as to what to do with/for them in a given situation. Children keep you honest. Because they haven't learned to dissemble, they challenge you with the truth. Children keep you joyful because of the miracle of their existence, the complexity of their emerging personalities, and the wonder of their learning about the world. Sometimes they make you proud.

Spiritual direction can help women to lift out and articulate this dimension of their spirituality.

It can also help them trust their sense that their path to God and style of prayer is rooted in these experiences. In *Motherhood and God*, Margaret Hebblethwaithe takes a very practical approach to this question.

So few of our major Christian exemplars in history have been mothers, and within my own, Catholic tradition so few are even today. There are also the problems of time and place that constitute a more complex obstacle course than any celibate adviser could dream possible. For the mother, it has to be a matter of personal experiment in a largely uncharted ground, and it is easy to lose heart and lose interest. And yet I believe the mother has special gifts and special privileges for her spiritual life that more than outweigh her practical difficulties.[11]

Finding this spiritual path takes time and encouragement, since the tradition provides little practical help, tending either to glorify motherhood or to ignore it. It is, as Hebblethwaite indicates, a matter of supporting women as they experiment with approaches to spirituality that fit the actual complexities and constraints of their lives, and as they learn to draw on the spiritual gifts to be found in those circumstances.

The mother/daughter cycle comes full circle in motherhood. But whether a woman chooses motherhood or not, the mother/daughter relationship is a powerful force in her spiritual life. This legacy, and its impact on her relationships with other women, is one that must be explored and healed if a woman is to move toward wholeness.

1. Reclaiming Our Heritage: Gathering Information

See if you can gather information on several generations of women in your family. Ask anyone who has some knowledge, and see how much you can piece together.

What were their religious affiliations, practices and convictions? Did they have favorite prayers and devotions? What values shaped their lives?

Notice any patterns you see repeated in your own life, or any parts of this legacy you have consciously rejected.

2. Women Who Have Influenced My Spiritual Life: An Exercise in Guided Imagination

Relax by getting in a comfortable position and breathing in and out deeply several times.

Now I want you to imagine yourself on a train platform in a train station . . . Train departures and arrivals are being announced . . . Take in the sights and sounds of the station . . .

You are waiting for a special train . . . Imagine the train coming toward you very slowly. On this train is a woman who has shaped your spiritual life in a positive way. She may be a relative or friend, a mother or spouse, a saint or biblical woman.

Stop the train now, and watch as a woman gets off the car to greet you. Who is she? Say anything you want to her. Now she talks to you. What does she say? Take a few minutes to talk about what she has meant in your spiritual life. When you have finished talking, say goodbye to the woman. Then see her turn and get back on the train. The train begins to move again, and you watch as it moves slowly on.

You stand for a few moments on the platform watching the train depart. Then you hear the sound of another train approaching in the distance. The train slows and stops. Another woman important in your spiritual life gets off. Who is she? Say anything you want to her. What does she say to you? Take a few minutes to talk with her. When you are finished, say goodbye to her. Watch her climb back on the train and move away in her car. Stand there a few moments as the train moves on.

Realize that you can bring back this train whenever you need to. Then quietly come back to this room.

3. The Prodigal Daughter: A Biblical Meditation

Language limits as well as expands our imagination and experience. As a way of bringing new insights into your reflection and prayer, paraphrase for yourself the story of the Prodigal Son in Luke 15:11–32 as the story of a Prodigal Daughter and her mother and sister. One way to do this is to change the gender of the main characters, i.e., father to mother, sons to daughters, and brothers to sisters. You may want to change other details as well.

NOTES

[1] A fine beginning is made in *Between Ourselves. Letters Between Mothers and Daughters*, ed. Karen Payne (Boston: Houghton Mifflin Company, 1983). See also Paula Gunn Allen, *The Sacred Hoop. Recovering the Feminine in American Indian Traditions* (Boston: Beacon Press, 1986); Signe Hammer, *Daughters and Mothers: Mothers and Daughters* (New York: New American Library, 1976).

[2] An example is Ronald W. Richardson, *Family Ties That Bind* (Vancouver, BC: International Self-Counsel Press, 1984).

[3] "Telling the Mother's Story: History and Connection in the Autobiographies of Maxine Hong Kingston and Kim Chernin," *Women's Studies* 14 (1987), 57–58. I am indebted to Barker-Nunn's analysis of these works.

[4] (New York: Anchor Press/Doubleday, 1984), p. 66.

[5] "Beyond the Oedipus Complex: Mothers and Daughters," *Work in Progress* (Wellesley, MA: Stone Center for Developmental Services and Studies, 1986), p. 15.

[6] (New York: Harper & Row, 1979).

[7] (New York: Harper & Row, 1976), p. 90.

[8] See, for example, Paula J. Caplan, *Barriers Between Women* (New York: Spectrum Publications, 1981).

[9] (New York: Alfred A. Knopf, 1985), p. 32. I am grateful to Cindy Fisher Rose for calling my attention to this poem.

[10] (Totowa, NJ: Rowman & Allanheld, 1983), pp. 1–4.

[11] (London: Geoffrey Chapman, 1984), p. 97.

Selected Bibliography

Andolsen, Barbara Hilkert, Christine E. Gudorf, and Mary D. Pellauer, eds. *Women's Consciousness, Women's Conscience. A Reader in Feminist Ethics.* San Francisco: Harper & Row, 1985.

Barry, William, and William Connolly. *The Practice of Spiritual Direction.* Minneapolis: Winston-Seabury, 1982.

Belenky, Mary Field, Blythe McVicker Clinchy, Nancy Rule Goldberger, and Jill Mattuck Tarule. *Women's Ways of Knowing. The Development of Self, Voice, and Mind.* New York: Basic Books, 1986.

Bynum, Caroline Walker. *Jesus As Mother. Studies in the Spirituality of the High Middle Ages.* Berkeley: University of California Press, 1982.

Christ, Carol P., and Judith Plaskow, eds. *Womanspirit Rising. A Feminist Reader in Religion.* San Francisco: Harper & Row, 1979.

Colledge, Edmund, O.S.A., and James Walsh, S.J., trans. *Julian of Norwich. Showings.* New York: Paulist Press, 1978.

Collins, Adela Yarbro, ed. *Feminist Perspectives on Biblical Scholarship.* Chico, CA: Scholars Press, 1985.

Conn, Joann Wolski, ed. *Women's Spirituality: Resources for Christian Development.* New York: Paulist Press, 1986.

212

Culligan, Kevin G., O.C.D., ed. *Spiritual Direction. Contemporary Readings.* Locust Valley, NY: Living Flame Press, 1983.

Craighead, Meinrad. *The Mother's Songs. Images of God the Mother.* New York: Paulist Press, 1985.

Dyckman, Katherine Marie, S.N.J.M., and L. Patrick Carroll, S.J. *Inviting the Mystic, Supporting the Prophet.* New York: Paulist Press, 1981.

Eck, Diana L. and Devaki Jain, eds. *Speaking of Faith. Global Perspectives on Women, Religion and Social Change.* Philadelphia: New Society Publishers, 1987.

Edwards, Tilden. *Spiritual Friend. Reclaiming the Gift of Spiritual Direction.* New York: Paulist Press, 1980.

Fiorenza, Elisabeth Schüssler. *In Memory of Her: A Feminist Theological Reconstruction of Christian Origins.* New York: Crossroad Publishing Co., 1983.

Fortune, Marie. *Sexual Violence. The Unmentionable Sin.* New York: The Pilgrim Press, 1983.

Gatta, Julia. *Three Spiritual Directors for Our Time: Julian of Norwich, The Cloud of Unknowing, Walter Hilton.* Cambridge, MA: Cowley Publications, 1986.

Gilligan, Carol. *In a Different Voice. Psychological Theory and Women's Development.* Cambridge, MA: Harvard University Press, 1982.

Greenspan, Miriam. *A New Approach to Women and Therapy.* New York: McGraw-Hill, 1983.

Hart, Thomas. *The Art of Christian Listening.* New York: Paulist Press, 1980.

Heyward, Isabel Carter. *The Redemption of God. A Theology of Mutual Relation.* Lanham, MD: University Press of America, 1982.

Janeway, Elizabeth. *Powers of the Weak.* New York: Alfred A. Knopf, 1980.

Kolbenschlag, Madonna. *Kiss Sleeping Beauty Good-Bye.* New York: Doubleday, 1979.

Lerner, Harriet. *The Dance of Anger.* New York: Harper & Row, 1985.

Larkin, Ernest. *Silent Presence: Discernment as Process and Problem.* Denville, NJ: Dimension Books, 1981.

Leech, Kenneth. *Soul Friend. The Practice of Christian Spirituality*. San Francisco: Harper & Row, 1977.

McAllister, Pam, ed. *Reweaving the Web of Life. Feminism and Nonviolence*. Philadelphia: New Society Publishers, 1982.

McFague, Sallie. *Models of God*. Philadelphia: Fortress Press, 1987.

Miller, Jean Baker. *Toward a New Psychology of Women*. Boston: Beacon Press, 1976.

Mollenkott, Virginia Ramey. *The Divine Feminine. The Biblical Imagery of God as Female*. New York: Crossroad Publishing Co., 1984.

Osiek, Carolyn. *Beyond Anger. On Being a Feminist in the Church*. New York: Paulist Press, 1986.

Pellauer, Mary D., Barbara Chester; and Jane Boyajian, eds. *Sexual Assault and Abuse: A Handbook for Clergy and Religious Professionals*. New York: Harper & Row, 1987.

Robbins, Joan Hamerman, and Rachel Josefowitz Siegel, eds. *Women Changing Therapy. New Assessments, Values and Strategies in Feminist Therapy*. New York: Harrington Park Press, 1985.

Rosewater, Lynne Bravo, and Lenore E.A. Walker, eds. *Handbook of Feminist Therapy. Women's Issues in Psychotherapy*. New York: Springer Publishing Co., 1985.

Ruether, Rosemary. *Sexism and God-Talk. Toward a Feminist Theology*. Boston: Beacon Press, 1983.

Russell, Letty M., ed. *Feminist Interpretation of the Bible*. Philadelphia: Westminster Press, 1985.

Russell, Letty M. *Household of Freedom. Authority in Feminist Theology*. Philadelphia: Westminster Press, 1987.

Schneiders, Sandra. *Women and the Word*. New York: Paulist Press, 1986.

Soelle, Dorothy. *The Strength of the Weak. Toward a Christian Feminist Identity*. Philadelphia: Westminster Press, 1984.

Tolbert, Mary Ann, ed. *The Bible and Feminist Hermeneutics. Semeia* 28. Chico, CA: Scholars Press, 1983.

Trible, Phyllis. *Texts of Terror. Literary-Feminist Readings of Biblical Narratives*. Philadelphia: Fortress Press, 1984.

Weaver, Mary Jo. *New Catholic Women. A Contemporary Challenge to Traditional Religious Authority.* San Francisco: Harper & Row, 1985.

Wehr, Demaris S. *Jung and Feminism. Liberating Archetypes.* Boston: Beacon Press, 1987.

Weidman, Judith L., ed. *Christian Feminism. Visions of a New Humanity.* San Francisco: Harper & Row, 1984.

Whitehead, Evelyn Eaton, and James D. Whitehead. *The Emerging Laity. Returning Leadership to the Community of Faith.* New York: Doubleday, 1986.

Wilson-Kastner, Patricia. *Faith, Feminism, and the Christ.* Philadelphia: Fortress Press, 1983.